A SPIRITED LIFE

The Life And Times Of Spirit Oquendo

MARY OQUENDO

WorkingChihuahua Press

WorkingChihuahua Press
Sequim, WA
www.SpiritedDog.com

Print ISBN 978-0-9828831-6-7
Ebook ISBN 978-0-9828831-7-4
Library of Congress Control Number: 2024901699
Copyright ©2024, WorkingChihuahua Press
Copyright information available upon request.
All rights reserved.

Front Cover Design: Get Covers
All images © the author unless otherwise stated.
Interior Design: Saloff Enterprises

Except in the United States of America, this book is sold subject to the condition that it shall not, by way of trade or otherwise, be lent, resold, hired out, or otherwise circulated without the publisher's prior consent in any form of binding or cover other than that in which it is published and without a similar condition including this condition being imposed on the subsequent purchaser.

The scanning, uploading and distribution of this book via the Internet or via any other means without permission of the publisher is illegal and punishable by law. Please purchase only authorized electronic editions, and do not participate in or encourage electronic piracy of copyrighted materials. Your support of the author's rights is appreciated.

v. 1.00
First Edition, 2024

Contents

Forward 1
Introduction 2
1. 2010 - The Beginning 3
2. My Second Home 6
3. 2011 - My Third Home 10
4. Meeting Mom #3 14
5. Meeting My New Dad 18
6. Going Home 21
7. Ghost Is a Stupid Name 24
8. 2012 - My Eyes Still Hurt 27
9. Unnecessary Body Parts 32
10. 2013 - Training Begins 36
11. 2014 - One Sexy Beast 41
12. Skunk Slayer 45
13. Trade Show Road Trip 48
14. Atlanta Pet Fair 54
15. I'm a Husky 58
16. Poke the Butt and My Stuff 63
17. The Smurf 66
18. 2016 - It's a Bad Day 71
19. Real Friends 73
20. Things I Dislike About Traveling to Classes and Trade Shows 79
21. I'm Annoyed 84
22. Hiking Off Leash 87
23. 2018 - My Brothers 91
24. 2019 - Moving Across the Country 95
25. 2020 - Retirement 101
26. Seizures and Declining Health 105
27. 2021 - Last Days 110
Acknowledgments 113

Foreword

When Mary told me about this project and asked me to help with early reads and feedback, I was looking forward to reading it as the tale unfolded. I also thought that this was primarily a way for someone who had loved deeply yet kept somewhat stoic to process her grief. I'd been there before and thought it was a way for her to pay tribute to a cherished pet who had touched her life so profoundly. Then I thought a bit more about Spirit and, more importantly, started reading.

In their loved person's eyes, every dog is amazing, but every so often, there comes an extra special pup, one who is destined to leave paw prints in the hearts and souls of everyone they meet. From trade shows to pet first aid classes, Spirit had the opportunity to better the lives of hundreds of people. Blessed to have been one of those people, I thought that time had passed for Spirit until I read his story. After living with a dog (or cat, bunny, or any pet, really), we get to know their unique personalities and voices. Even having had the privilege of knowing Spirit, I felt like I got to know him better through this book.

This exceptional story is told from the perspective of the only one who really knew what Spirit was going through and that's Spirit himself. I won't argue the controversy of whether he actually narrated this book to his "mom," (because he without doubt did), but I will say that through this heartwarming tail his legacy of joy lives on.

This is a must-read if you've ever wondered what goes on inside of an exceptional dog —or any dog's head. But enough of this, let's hear what the Good Boy himself has to say.

~ Chris Anthony, Owner, Groomer,
Have Shears Will Travel

Introduction

Hi! Wait, I think Mom says 'ellow. That sounds right. Ellow!

Let me introduce myself. My name is Spirit, and I'm a white Siberian Husky. I've been blind since birth thanks to glaucoma and I'm toothless due to my distemper. Plus, I have painful hips because my Mom was overbred at a puppy mill. None of which has ever slowed me down or made me feel sorry for myself. I'm not handicapped, but as you'll see, I'm differently abled.

Life is to be lived to the fullest. As I feel I'm getting close to the end of my incredible life, I want to inspire those around me to live fully. I could not be who I am without the love and support from all my families. As much as I would love to write down everything, there simply isn't time. Squeakies need my attention! These are the highlights and whatever I found important to me.

The timeline is not equal between chapters. I've lived a lot and don't 'member it all!

I did ask Mom to proofread for spelling and grammatical errors, as well as keep track of my timeline because I can't be good at everything!

Without further ado, here's my story.

Spirit Oquendo

Chapter 1

2010 - The Beginning

It was a dark and stormy night…haha, wrong book!

I wish I could describe my first weeks, but all I could see were shadows. It was all gray and blobby. That's the best way to describe it: gray and blobby. I never felt well, and my head always hurt to some degree. While the place I lived was cramped, there was a comfort in being so close to my mother and siblings. A couple of my littermates died. That was terrible; I couldn't move away from their bodies. When one of the Others came to refill our food, their bodies were removed.

Right from the start, I knew I was different from my family. While we all could see, we saw differently. My family could see the physical. They saw our home, each other, the Others who filled our food and water, and the barrier that prevented us from playing with the other dogs. I saw essences, and I felt things. I felt my mother licking me, nudging me to eat, and snuggling with me to keep me warm. Looking back, I've always wondered if my mom ever got the opportunity to have a family like I eventually did. I sure hope so. My mother was beautiful, though my brother said she didn't look well. I saw my brother and sister as vibrant. I always knew where they began and ended.

I had fun with my brother and sister. The most fun we had was when we were trying to escape. We'd all take turns trying to climb out—even me! My brother succeeded one time. He climbed the fence that surrounded our home, but a couple of hours later, he was brought back and tossed over the fence by one of the Others. The Others were mostly quiet, but they did something to the fence and for the first time, I heard them speak. In an angry voice, one Other said "Try that again, will ya!"

That was the first time I saw sharp edges around an essence.

My brother climbed that fence again, and he yelped. My brother said he had fun anyway. He told me we lived in one of many plastic igloos, and we got to meet so many other dogs. I knew that. I could smell all of them.

It seemed like this was where I would live forever.

I was happy to be with my family, but it was getting a little cramped, plus I still wasn't feeling well, but I just thought this was life. One day, I noticed my mother's essence getting smaller. I could feel her sadness, and that's when the Others picked up my siblings and me and took us away from our mother. For the first time, I was alone in a box away from my family. I knew they were around me, along with many other dogs, but I was all by myself. I didn't know it at the time, but it was the last time I would be with my family. The box I was in was lifted up, and I felt myself sliding until my box hit another box. It was dark, and my eyes and head hurt. My brother said we were in a big truck. He sounded brave, but I could see that he, along with everyone else, was scared. I was too.

Suddenly, I felt a presence in my crate, and at first, I didn't understand how they got into my box as I was alone. It felt like another dog seemed to take up all the space while not taking up any room. She told me her name was Kira, and I could feel warmth and comfort. She said she would stay with me for a while and to have faith that everything would be okay. Boy, I sure hoped everyone in the truck heard that! I heard something that sounded like doors closing, and then my box shook a little. I felt movement, but I wasn't moving. My brother was keeping all of us informed as to what was happening. Kira was telling me stories about her family. It sounded wonderful. I hoped me and my brother and sister would have a family like hers.

Every so often, movement would stop, and I heard the doors open. Someone would take a couple of crates out and remark on how stinky we were. My brother got off on the first stop, and now I didn't have anyone to tell me what was happening. My sister was removed on the third stop. I never saw my mother, brother, or sister after that. My eyes and head were hurting, my stomach hurt, and now my butt was sore. Another Other took my crate off the truck at the fourth stop and placed it on the ground.

"You're all so cute!" I heard a girl squeal. She brought all of us inside a building. Once inside, the Squealy Girl picked me up and said, "You're the cutest, but stinky. I'm going to give you a bath!" She was an Other, but she wasn't. She felt wonderful.

So, let me tell you what a bath is! They get you wet and rub you down so lovely, tell you you're a good boy, and rub you down some more. For the first time since they took me away from my family, I wasn't so scared anymore.

That is until a different Other starts yelling, "What the FUCK!? Why did you accept this dog? Do you see his eyes? How the hell can I sell a blind dog? Now I have to get the pink juice and fill out a bunch of forms!" He scared me. I think I peed a little. He was all sharp edges. What's pink juice anyway?

"I'll take him! I'll pay what he costs you, and I'm going to take him home with me," Squealy Girl said.

The Other bellowed, "You have no idea what you're getting yourself into!"

"I don't care. His name is Po, and I'm taking him home!"

And home I went.

Mary's note: *I know I'm supposed to just be your spell checker, but I'm just going to say it. Fuck them all. You were born in a puppy mill and sent to be sold. None of them deserved to have you. Except Squealy Girl.*

Chapter 2

My Second Home

The place where I was first brought to by the truck was where Squealy Girl worked. I learned that working is what you do to get money to buy things. As she was getting ready to take me home, the Other started to sound a little whiny. "Where are you going? What do you think you're doing taking all these things? I don't see you paying for it," he said as Squealy Girl was lifting me into her car.

Squealy Girl told him that since he didn't pay her enough, plus it was about time he did something nice for someone else, this was his contribution to my wellbeing. She couldn't afford a nice bed or toys for me. For a minute, the sharp spikes around the Other rounded a bit. But, they went right back to spikes when he said, "Only because I can charge it back to the manufacturer as damaged goods. It's a one-time deal."

This was way different from the truck I was in earlier that day. It didn't feel so constrained, but Squealy Girl had to move things out of the way to make room for me. I heard all sorts of things hitting the ground as she was apologizing for the mess in the backseat. It didn't feel like I was in a box, and I could feel the air! Who knew that air had a feel to it?

Boy, her place smells nice—not like any of the places I've been before. I smell… food? Is that what food smells like? I never smelled food before. It never had a smell, or a taste for that matter, at my first home. Because I can't see, my other senses work overtime. The floor is soft, but ouch! Lots of obstacles. Some are hard. I'm told to watch for walls, tables, and chairs. Usually the warning comes after I walk into them. Then, Squealy Girl tells me what it is, rubs my head, and tells me I'm gonna need some aspirin. I hope aspirin tastes like chicken. I like chicken. I don't mind bumping into soft things like the sofa. Good thing they all smell different; it didn't take me long to figure out where everything was.

"Hey, Po, this is your bed! You'll sleep here." Squealy Girl hugged me and told me she loves me. I have my own bed. I hope my brother and sister have such a great place to live like me.

Sometimes the floor is not there! I'm told that they are steps. I don't like them but, I gotta do the steps when she takes me outside for walks. Walks are amazing! So many smells! I get to meet other dogs and Others that don't have spiky edges.

After a couple of weeks, Kira told me I was going to break Squealy Girl's heart. She told me this was just the first stop for me. I told her that I was good with this soft bed, two meals a day, all the water I could drink, and being hugged. And did you see my squeaky? Squeak squeak squeak! I love this. I love Squealy Girl! She says she's now my Mom. She's my second Mom. Boy, Moms are good. I hope my other Mom is okay. I miss her.

My head and stomach hurts. Mom rubs my head when I sit on her lap or she's cleaning me up because all I do is poop. My butt hurts too. Mom says she's going to talk to a friend of hers who can make me feel better.

One day, I hear the doorbell ring, and I run to the door and alert Mom to the intruder. Gotta pull my weight around here! Plus, I get head rubs before she opens the door. Win-win!

"Hey, Po. This is my friend Kaeley, and she's just going to look you over."

And she did. She knew everything that hurt; she spoke so softly to me. Then, I listened as she spoke with my Mom.

"Listen, Julie—he's a very sick boy. He has glaucoma. His eyes and head must be killing him. Something's up with his teeth, and I suspect he has giardia, which by the way, is a zoonotic disease. If you start having digestive issues, I'd recommend you see a doctor. It's going to cost tens of thousands of dollars to get him healthy."

I can hear Mom crying. I have the 'coma, and I may be making my Mom sick. This is really bad.

"I'm sorry, Julie. I know how much you love him. I have an option for you. Surrender him to my vet hospital. As long as he becomes the office dog, the vet hospital will eat the costs of his treatment. I have a yearly budget for this type of situation. But, he has to be the property of the vet hospital. I will not be able to give him back to you once he's healthy. The sooner we do this, the better it will be for both of you. I'd also replace this rug if he pooped on it."

Kira came back and told me to get ready for stop number two. They will get me healthy so I can go onto my final stop. She told me to get ready for visits from 3 ghosts… haha wrong story again! What she told me was that Marcus would be helping me from here on out. I asked Kira why only I seemed to acknowledge her. She told me that I'm special and only I can hear her. I wanted her to stay, but she said that all I had to do was think of her and I'd feel her.

Mom was crying as she loaded up all my stuff. I have stuff to bring! My bed and squeakies—she had to use a large plastic bag. Mom hugged and kissed me. I'm going to miss her. I love her so much. Mom told me to be a good boy for Kaeley, that she will miss me and will think of me always. I broke her heart just like Kira said I would. I saw my second Mom's essence get smaller just like my first Mom's did.

Now, Kaeley's car was much bigger than Mom's and I had to be picked up. Kaeley put me in a crate in the back of her vehicle, and she apologized for putting a plastic sheet in the crate over the bed. It was slippy, and I slid a little whenever Kaeley took a corner. She drives faster than Mom does (LOL).

And for the third time, I was going for a ride.

Chapter 3

2011 - My Third Home

When the car stopped, Kaeley said we had to go in the back door, and I had to go into "ice solation" (huh?) because I may be 'tagious and get other dogs sick. I don't want to do that—I want to be a good neighbor. Kaeley introduced me to Kristin.

"Hey there, cutie pie. You and I are going to be great friends!" Kristin was all round and soft.

It sure is noisy here. As soon as we walked in, all these dogs started to bark. Kaeley said they are boarders and here temporarily while their owners are away on vacation. I knew that because most of them were asking me if I saw their people in the parking lot. People? Oh, that's the real name for Others. Once past the noise, I recognized the smell of soap and heard machines going. It smelled the same as my bed when Mom cleaned it when I pooped on it. I didn't want to poop on it, but I couldn't get outside fast enough. I hope my Mom is doing ok. I like Kaeley, she tells me everything I'm about to do. This place is so much different than any place I've been before. I don't know what to expect.

"We're going to go up the stairs. I'm going to walk behind you, so you're going first."

There were so many stairs. I thought there were 3 or 4 stairs; there were like hundreds of stairs.

"Good job, Po. I know 20 stairs is a lot."

There's so many people here! I got lots of pets. I hope I remember all their names.

"This is your special medical crate. There is always someone nearby who can see you and help you during the day."

Oooh, I have a special crate, and my bed is already here. How'd that get here so fast? All my squeakies too!

Lots of differences between this and my last home. Most of the time, I live in a small place they call a medical crate. It smells so different. It's almost like where I was born, except it's nice and warm. There are so many people who hug me. I have my own special place to walk when I go outside. I can't go to the play yard until I'm no longer 'tagious. They let me roam around the vet hospital before they open up for sick pets. There are so many hard things to bump into. There's a ton of counters and exam tables everywhere. It's a maze. I always make sure they close the door to the steps by going to check on it. Haha, somebody always runs past me to make sure it's closed.

The first day I was there, I met Dr. P. Everybody here just calls him "P." Kristin picked me up and put me on one of the exam tables.

"Let's go over Po with a fine-tooth comb to make sure we know what's going on and set up a treatment plan for him."

Well, it turns out, it isn't just a comb! There are needles involved. I didn't like those. It turns out my treatment plan includes some gross pills and needles.

I'm told this is a place to make sick animals better. I'm sick and they're trying to make me better. My stomach and butt feel better, but my eyes still hurt. I listen to them when they talk about me. They said I had distemper, giardia, and glaucoma. I don't think they know about the 3rd home, as they want me to be part of their business as soon as I'm better.

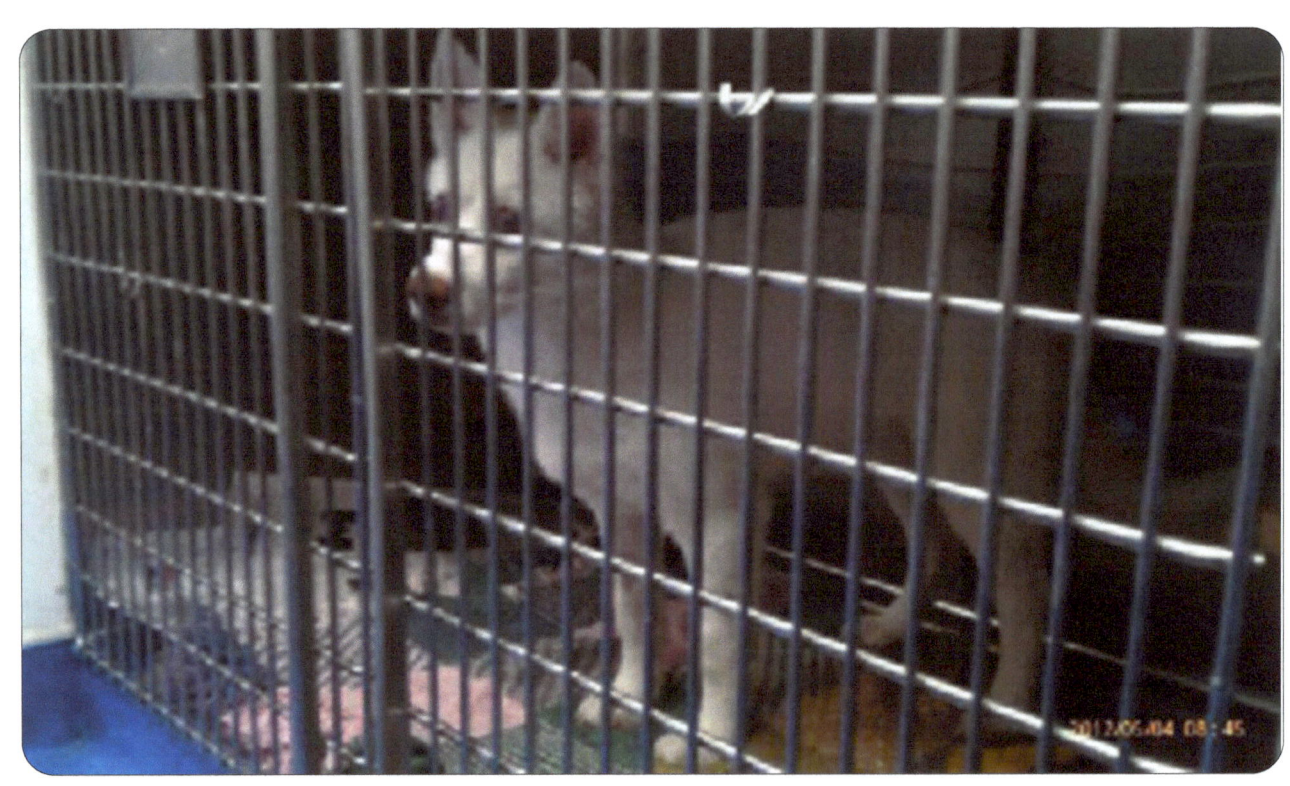

Me in my special medical crate at the vet's.

They have cats here! They're small, furry, and very fast. I like cats. They play with me. My favorite game is tag! They tag me with their paws and run away. Then, I have to find them and tag them. They're really teaching me my way around this place and showing me where all the good hiding spots are.

The people here call me the fish dog. I don't know what that means.

"You're the office dog, not a fish dog," a presence whispered in my ear. This must be the Marcus that Kira was telling me about. That makes much better sense than being a fish. Though, they do bathe me a lot! The novelty of the bath is starting to wear off. But I now know what a comb is, and I don't see how this can tell how my health is.

I thought Marcus would be bigger; his energy feels huge. It turns out he's a Miniature Pinscher.

"Fuck you, I'm a Maximum Pinscher! I'm going to teach you something. It's called a head tilt, and it's my signature move. It will get you to your final home. I will let you know when to do it, so don't do it until I tell you to."

Note to self—Don't be snarky with Marcus until I'm home. He's a little sensitive. He's also a little bossy.

While it seemed really silly, we practiced and practiced until I got it right. And then, Marcus told me to be patient.

After being here awhile, I learned that there are more People than Others. They are pretty easy to tell apart. Others are all spiky and People have softer edges. I like People better.

2011 - My Third Home

Chapter 4

Meeting Mom #3

I get to play in the play yard since I'm no longer 'tagious. The play yard is awesome! The ground is soft and tickles my paws sometimes. I get to run and chase a ball, and sometimes I play with other dogs!!! The only downsides to the play yard are the trees. There are eight of them—ask me how I know that. I did learn pretty quickly that trees also have energy around them. Once I learned to sense them, I stopped running into trees. I veer off at the very last second, which causes, as I'm told, a near heart attack for Kristin and Chrystal.

Marcus has been very helpful even though he'd probably deny it. He used to have sight before he went blind, so he tried to explain colors to me. But what he really taught me was that everything has either a smell, a sound, or a buzz. And the different combinations of the three tells me who and where they are. What I called spiky and round edges, Marcus called buzzing. People smell different and sometimes talk in different pitches, but their personal buzz is pretty consistent. I know where the trees are in the play yard because of their buzz and smell, so I no longer run into them while running. I can tell when the cats want to play with me or when they want me to leave them alone by the sounds they make. Hahaha makes no difference to me whether or not they WANT to play!

One morning, I was sleeping in my crate when Marcus literally screamed in my ear. "She just parked her car. Get up right now and act like you're going to poop. Showtime, baby!"

You'd be surprised how fast a person can move when they think you're going to poop.

I was leashed up and out the door in less than 10 seconds. I like Kristin. She's a vet tech that spends a lot of time with me. I'm going to miss her.

I sensed a lady walking up the driveway; she stopped to talk to Kristin. Her edges were very rounded, but she sounded a little sad. Marcus said she was sad because of him. He was her Love Bug.

Boy, can these two can talk. It took me 8 head tilts to get her attention.

"Oh my god! He just tilted his head the same way Marcus used to do."

My mom-to-be's voice sounded very nice and I could tell she had other dogs that lived with her.

"Whose dog is he?"

Kristin told her that I was the fish, I mean, office dog.

She asked if I was up for adoption and Kristin said absolutely. But apparently, there are two hurdles I had to overcome. One was my health and the other was someone named Ernesto. We had to convince him. I could tell by the way they were whispering and giggling that this was just about a done deal. I was a little worried that she would be afraid to take me home because of all the things that were wrong with me.

Marcus got very smug with me and said, I told you so. He also told me I was no longer welcome to use the head tilt. He wished me luck and said I was "in like flynn," whatever that means. He said Ernesto was really a push over, and that he'll have a conversation with Ricky to make sure everything goes smoothly.

My new Mom comes to visit me a lot and brings me new toys. Okay, okay, okay, I know technically she's not officially my Mom, but I know in my heart that it's the final home that Kira was telling me about.

16 | *Meeting Mom #3*

Did I tell you I love squeakies? Sometimes it's a ball! I love balls almost as much as I do squeakies because I can chase after them in the play yard.

I always know when Mom is coming to visit because Kristin puts on my new collar and leash. I'm told that I look handsome. Me and Mom sit outside and she feeds me the best snackies. She tells me all about my new brothers—Reno, Baby, and Ricky. Reno is blind like me and Ricky works with her. Baby is the King.

She also tells me about Ernesto. He seems nice, but I have to win him over. Challenge accepted! I love my new Mom and want to go home.

I'm counting on Ricky to get me home.

Ricky's note: *I will be so glad to get Po here. Reno has been such a grump ever since he went blind. He doesn't want to play or go for a walk or anything except complain that he can't see anything anymore. Marcus has been keeping me updated on Po's progress. I'm confident that we can convince Ernesto.*

Chapter 5

Meeting My New Dad

I was so excited! Marcus told me about my three other brothers and my dad. So far, I've had three moms, but Ernesto was going to be my first Dad. Marcus said that Dad does not know how to talk in soft tones, but is a pushover. It wouldn't take long to train him. He'd do anything for us, including something called debt. I understand that's what happens when one of us gets sick and Dad has to work extra to pay the debt to make us better.

Reno is the blind German Pinscher. Mom and Dad call him the coffee table. Hahaha apparently a couple of books would fit on his back. Reno would eat anything and even though he complains he can't see, he always finds the food. Baby is a Chihuahua. He's under the impression that he's in charge. He's the boss, but to be clear, he was never the boss of me. Ricky is a Golden Retriever. Everything is by the rules with him. His favorite saying is, "That's not how we do things here" and, "You'd better behave while I'm traveling with Mom." Little did he know that Dad totally spoiled us whenever Mom and Ricky were working. We got cooked chicken, extra treats, and more cooked chicken!

All the women in the vet office were excited as well. They continually told Dr. P. to let them work it out, they had a plan, and he was not to screw it up. I liked Dr. P. He was the only veterinarian there. He told me that we were outnumbered here, and us guys had to stick together.

The plan, as I understood it, was that my new Mom and Dad were going to bring one of my brothers in for a 'pointment. Then, Kristin was going to casually walk in the 'pointment room with this cute little blind Husky (that's me) on her way in from a walk and she and Mom would talk a bit (nothing surprising or out of the ordinary there as Mom and Kristen always talked) while Ricky (my brother) and me interacted. After Dad agreed I would be a good addition, Dr. P. would come in to see Ricky and act all surprised.

Today's the day, I'm so nervous. (I pooped 3 times!) As soon as Mom and Dad and Ricky got here, Kristin and me ever so casually walked into the exam room (that's what they call the 'pointment room), and Kristen started to tell Mom and Dad about me.

She talked about how I was 'rendered to them because of all my medical conditions and how they didn't think they would be able to find me a home. Cue the violins: I would have to live the rest of my life here at the hospital. All the while, me and Ricky were playing.

Me and Ricky casually playing while mom and Kristin talked.

I know that Dad was taking it all in. He was looking at Mom and Kristin, and then at me and Ricky, 'cause I could feel his eyes on me and then not on me, and then on me again.

I'll admit, I got a little scared listening to how bad I had it. But Ricky said, "Son, we all have a story. My first family gave me up because I had so

Meeting My New Dad | 19

much energy. I was headed to the shelter before Mom intervened and took me home. Your brother, Reno, was brought to this very hospital when his first Mom died. He was very anxious and they weren't sure they would be able to adopt him out. We were being boarded and when Mom and Dad came to pick us up, Dad took one look at Reno and heard his story. Reno came home with us that very day. Relax, this is handled." Even Baby had a previous home before he came to live with Mom and Dad. I love my big brother. And he is big, much bigger than me. I know why they call him a Golden Retriever. He is gold!

As Kristin and Mom talked, the other ladies that worked there would walk in and comment on how well me and Ricky were playing. Or how cute I was, and they hoped they would find me a real home soon.

Then, Dr. P. walked in the room.

"Hey guys, thanks so much for adopting Po. It will be a couple months though. We need to get him healthy enough to leave. We want to make sure that giardia is cleared up, so that it doesn't affect your other dogs. His eyes are going to be the biggest issue. We can treat his glaucoma here, but you may want to see a specialist. I do have a recommendation."

You could have heard a pin drop as everyone stopped and turned to look at P., including me and Ricky. I hoped Dr. P. didn't just screw up my chances. I mean Dad had just been sitting there, not saying anything but looking at me, then Ricky, then Mom and Kristen, back to me again.

I was so relieved when Dad said, "Well, none of you were fooling me. We'll take the blind Husky. However, Po is a dumb name and we'll call him Ghost."

Good to know that Dad is pretty smart! Actually, Ghost is a dumb name as well, but I'm sure we can take care of that down the line. I could tell Mom agreed with me as well.

Chapter 6

Going Home

Very exciting day today! It feels different than when Mom comes to visit me. She comes often, and we sit outside with my squeaky and discuss the meaning of life while she feeds me the nectar of the gods: cheese. Cheese is glorious. I never had it before. I just don't like cheese, I LOVE cheese! Anyway, the office is abuzz today. They packed my stuff and set it by the receptionist counter. Apparently, the parasite that has been living inside of me is now dead. 'Bout time. Freeloader. It was keeping me from going home.

They just told me that Mom is coming to bring me home!!!! I'm so excited I have to go pee again. BRB.

Getting ready to leave the vets with all my stuff.

Everyone here is crying and has presents for me. So many new squeakies! Dr. P. gave me the man-to-man talk. He told me to be good and not let Baby walk all over me. He said he wasn't crying, someone left onions all over his office. Then Kaeley came over and said that this wasn't goodbye as me and my brothers will be back for boarding when Mom and Dad go on vacation. And she doesn't know what Dr. P. is talking about, there are no onions in his office. Haha, I knew that.

Mom is here! Everyone is clapping. The cats must be very upset that I'm leaving, because they are all hiding. Even Kira and Marcus are here to see me off. Dad was waiting in the car and had to help me get into the car and in my crate. They should have brought a bigger car. I have so much stuff!

It seemed like it took forever to get to my final home. Ooh, it smells so different here! I smell trees and grass and other dogs. Dad took off my collar and leash. Ricky came running up to me, "Son, welcome home, let me introduce you to your brothers. Baby is the patriarch of the family. He's really old. He's little, but mighty."

Baby: That's right, I'm a mighty Chihuahua. We are the ruling class. I'm in charge here. Don't use the 'I can't see' and run into me. You can smell and see where I'm at. I will rip your ear off if you run over me. Welcome to the family!

I can see what Dr. P. was talking about. Baby is a little scary.

Ricky: This is Reno. He's blind like you. He's a grouch and has no sense of humor.

Reno: Be careful in the backyard. There's a fence, but I can't see it or the trees, and you don't want to run into a tree. Take it nice and easy. I don't see anything funny about not being able to see. It's very unfair. I'm a German Pinscher,

Me meeting Reno for the first time.

I come from a long line of stoic ancestors. If you don't act all crazy, none of us will get hurt.

Oooookaaay.

There's so much room here. I can run! I'm gonna run. Bonk! Oh, that must be a tree. Bonk! That must be the fence. Haha! The headache is going to be worth it. Bonk! Ricky ran with me. He was trying to warn me about the bonkables, but I'm too fast. I could hear Baby laughing and made a comment about Huskies not being too bright. I beg to disagree Baby. I'm literally vibrating with joy! I bet my edges are glowing and are indeed very bright. Reno was shouting at me to be careful, as I almost ran into him a couple of times. I was real careful about not running into Baby.

It won't take me long to figure this out. Wait, do I smell cheese? There's cheese here! I was wondering where Mom got her supply. I stopped so quickly that Ricky ran into me.

Ricky: Why'd you stop?

Spirit: I smell cheese.

Ricky: Oh yeah, Mom wants us to come in. She's shaking the bag of cheese. Follow me!

Mom put the collar and leash back on me and said we needed to go up the stairs. I hate stairs, but if it's leading to cheese, point me in the right direction! My new home is almost like my second Mom's home. All sorts of hard things like tables and chairs and soft things like sofa and beds. Boy, there are a lot of beds here.

Baby made it real clear which bed was his.

Baby: See this bed here?

Spirit: No.

Baby: Don't be an ass. This one. The one I'm standing on. The one that smells like me. This is my bed. You can use any of the others, but not this one.

I love my new family, even Baby.

Chapter 7

Ghost Is a Stupid Name

Before we get into why Ghost is a stupid name, let me tell you about the conversation I just overheard.

Dad talking to Mom: *What did you do with the cheese I left on the table?*
Mom: *What do you mean what did I do with your cheese? I did nothing with your cheese.*
Dad: *You must have. I put some chunks on the counter and now they're gone.*
Mom: *Seriously. You put cheese on the counter and are wondering where it went.*
LOL Mom turned to look at me. She's much smarter than Dad.
Dad: *Ricky never takes anything off the counter, and the other dogs are too small or blind.*
Mom: *While you're thinking about that, go smell Ghost's breath. That Husky nose of his works just fine.*

It was a little difficult to follow this conversation as I was engaged in another at the same time.

Ricky: Did you eat the cheese?
Me: It was just sitting there on the table. Of course, I did!
Reno: You didn't! You're not supposed to take food off the table. Now Dad has no cheese to share with us.
Me: It was delicious, and I have no regrets. Cheese magically appears here all the time. What's the problem?
Baby: We need to have a discussion. If I could have reached the table, all the cheese would be gone and I would have zero regrets as well. However, since I can't, neither can you.

Me: I beg to differ, I can and will eat the cheese.

Baby: Let me clarify. Eat the cheese and that results in me not getting any cheese, and I will end you.

Me: Ohkay. What if I knock a piece on the floor for you?

Baby: Acceptable.

Reno: Hey!

I love cheese. Now you see why Dad should not be in charge of my name. Ghost is a scary name, and I'm more of a lover. This discussion between Mom and Dad has been going on for a while. Dad's not budging on my name—something about some TV show that he watches. There's a Dire Wolf called Ghost that reminds Dad of me. Now, I don't mind being confused for a Dire Wolf, they're pretty cool. But we're coming down to the wire! Once my name goes on the tag, it's a done deal. You can't change the tag! (I don't even know what the tag is.)

Me: Hey, Ricky, what's this tag thing that is so important?

Ricky: It's a special decoration that has your name and Mom's name and a phone number. In case you get lost and someone finds you, they can call Mom to come get you. It's official. Mom has to register us with the city. In case that person brings you to the shelter instead or the police find you, then Mom won't have to pay a fine.

Me: What are police?

Baby: He means the Po Po. If they find you, they throw you in the pokey! The pokey is where they keep all the bad people. You don't want to go there. There's no cheese there. But on a positive note, there'd be more cheese for me.

Ricky: Don't listen to him. The police look out for you and would bring you home. Back to the tag. I got lost one day. I saw a deer and something came over me and I jumped the fence and ran after it. I didn't know where I was. I was so scared! This nice lady saw me in her yard and came over and petted me and called Mom. It was Dad that picked me up as he was driving around looking for me. I was so glad I had the tag!

Dad wasn't budging on the name so Mom had to bring out the big guns. She called Karen. Karen is an animal communicator and a friend of Mom's. Karen talks to me and then tells Mom and Dad what I said. It was really weird the first time Karen was in my head. I was looking around for her, but she wasn't there. I told Karen I didn't like the name Ghost. I didn't want people to think I was dead. Ghosts are dead. Ghosts are scary. Karen told Mom who told Dad. Dad was all remorseful. He felt bad. I told Karen, I would rather be called Spirit.

So everybody, I'm Spirit now!!!!

Chapter 8

2012 - My Eyes Still Hurt

Ricky: Spirit! Spirit! The Littles are here. I love the Littles.

Spirit: What are Littles?

Ricky: Mom's grandkids. She says they're better than her kids. I agree. The Littles throw the ball for hours.

Baby: Jeez, I'll be in my crate. Someone lock the door. Don't bother me unless they're dropping food on the floor.

Spirit: They drop food on the floor and throw balls! Yeah, okay, Baby. I'll let you know if they drop food.

I could tell that Ricky wasn't going to let Baby know anything either. The real issue was beating Reno to the food. For a fat, whiny, blind dog, he sure could move fast when food hit the floor!

Who knew Littles could cause such chaos? Hahaha! Food on the floor and all the stuff they needed. There was so much stuff. Bags with food, bags with toys, bags with who knows what? Mom made the formal introductions. While it seemed like a hundred Littles, there were only three. The biggest was Tyler who threw the ball for Ricky. Ricky could chase after a ball for hours. Dad says he throws the ball for Ricky until his arm falls off. I wonder how he reattaches his arm all the time? Are people's arms removable? I hadn't noticed before. Anyway, Gavin was my favorite. He just hugged me. Gavin threw the ball for me, but because he was so little, it only went about 6 inches. But I made a big deal of chasing it and gave it back to him. I never heard anyone giggle before. I loved the way it sounded. Plus, he's a sloppy eater. I'm not sure Violet really counts as she's so

Gavin loves me.

small she's not allowed on the floor to play with us. Mom was hovering. She was telling them to be careful around my eyes as they hurt.

Which reminds me. My eyes do still hurt because of the 'coma.

Mom can explain it better than I can.

Mary's note: *I'm going to get all scientific on you because It's important you know what it is and how to notice it on your pets.*

It's called Glaucoma. It occurs when there is high pressure in the eyes and normal outflow of fluid within the eye is impaired.

It can be caused by:
- Improper development of the eye's filtration angles. (primary)
- Eye diseases such as: primary lens luxation, inflammation of the tissues of the eye, eye tumor, or blood collection in the front of the eye from injury. (secondary)

In Spirit's case, he was born with it. He never really had vision, mostly just greyed out shapes.

Symptoms may appear in any combination of:

- High pressure
- Eye blinking
- Receding eyeball
- Redness
- Cloudy appearance
- Dilated pupil
- Pupil does not respond to light
- Vision loss
- Enlarged eyeball (buphthalmos)
- Visible debris
- Constricted pupil
- Iris sticking to either the cornea or the lens
- Headaches
- Loss of appetite
- Change in attitude

Sometimes it can be treated with special eye drops, but not all the time. If drops don't help, then enucleation is the only option. It's a surgical procedure that removes the eyes.

Okay, thanks Mom! My eyes were huge and hurt all the time. Mom took me to the Animal Eye Clinic in Wilton, CT. I like this place. They met us at the door and walked us into the building, making sure I knew where I was at all times. Everybody there was so nice to me and spoke gently to me, just like Kaeley did when she met me for the first time at my second Mom's house. That's how I knew it was something serious. They kept telling me I was a good boy, and they had snackies. Reno would be jealous. I'll make sure to let him know how many snackies I got! The doctor tested my eyes with a big thing and announced I had the 'coma. Yeah, we already knew that. The doctor gave my mom some drops to put in my eyes he said might help.

Reno was pretty pissed when I got home and told him all about the snackies. Mom put him on a diet, and he can only have baby carrots as a snackie. Reno doesn't even like carrots, but he eats them anyway. Mom says Reno would eat the wallpaper off the wall if he could, which is why she puts him in a crate to eat so that he doesn't shove the rest of us out of the way to eat our delicious food. So, of course, we all eat extra slowly. Reno is so easy to mess with. Hahaha!

    Anyway, twice a day, Mom put drops in my eyes. I don't like it, but I know she's trying to help. Unfortunately, they did not help at all. The next step is to remove my eyes so they will stop hurting. I'm all in. Anything to make the headaches go away!

Chapter 9

Unnecessary Body Parts

Now that the decision has been made to remove my eyes, I'm starting to get a little nervous. Mom and Dad decided that Dr. P. would do the surgery to remove my eyeballs. I'm getting worried because everyone at the hospital is talking in that soft, "it's going to be alright" tone of voice. I'm really starting to dislike it.

I thought Ricky would be able to offer some words of wisdom because he knows everything. It turns out, he doesn't. My mind is blown! He's never had major surgery.

Ricky: I'm sorry. I wish I could tell you what's going to happen, but I have no experience here.

But help came from an unexpected source. Baby, all six pounds of him, just muscled Ricky out of the way.

Baby: I've had major surgery. But first, let me tell you why I had to have surgery.

Ricky: How many times do I have to say I'm sorry, Baby? It was an accident. I didn't mean to do it.

Baby: Until the pain has been erased from my memory. So, never! Anyway. Here I am, sleeping peacefully under the blanket when the next thing I know, I'm being ripped in half.

Ricky: I was playing tug of war with Marcus. We couldn't find the tug toy, so we each grabbed an end of the blanket. We didn't know you were there!

Baby: 15 stitches, Ricky. 15 stitches! Anyway, Mom rushed me over to the hospital, and they stitched me up. Did I say it was 15 stitches? I went home the next day and had to take so many pills, which I hate. They put The Cone on me. But on the flip side, I got the Costco chicken with skin.

Reno: Yeah, The Cone was pretty funny. It was probably as big as Baby is and took up half the hallway space. Baby made Ricky sqwoosh himself against the wall to go past him. Didn't think Ricky could flatten himself that much.

Spirit: The Cone?

Baby: It's to prevent you from licking or biting at your stitches. Really important when you have 15 of them.

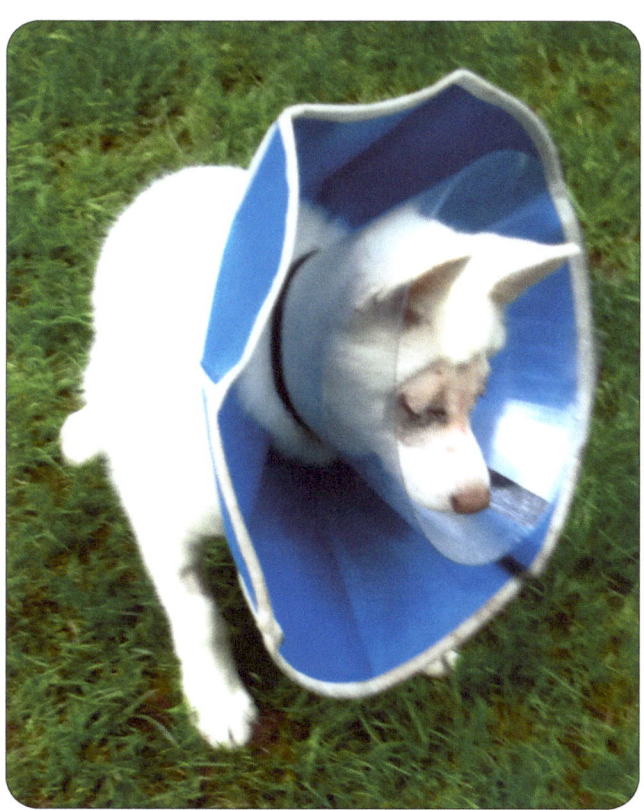

Anyway! I couldn't have brekkfuss the morning of surgery. Which I suppose is a good thing as I might have thrown it up. After surgery, Dr. P. said they were going to sew buttons on my face and everyone laughed, but they didn't do it. Bummer. My head still hurts a bit, but I'm assured it's now temporary as I recover from surgery. What is really annoying is this thing they put on me so I don't bump my head and open up my stitches. The Cone. I hate it. It's stupid. I keep banging it on the sides of walls and doors. It's hard to eat! And for some reason everyone laughs when I do. Even Ricky and the grump Reno are

Unnecessary Body Parts

snickering. Haha, so funny. I have to fit The Cone around the bowl and then stretch a bit so my mouth reaches the bowl. Apparently, it's hilarious. I'm not amused.

Dr. P. was right! My head no longer hurts and they took The Cone off. It was a glorious day. I got a get-well present. It was a new squeaky! I love it. Squeak! Squeak! Squeak! I don't let Ricky go near my squeakies. All he wants to do is destroy and remove the squeaky. It's no fun if it doesn't squeak! His squeakies don't even last a day. Brothers. Plus, I got all the cheese I could eat.

Anyway, when I got the OK to remove The Cone, Kaely put googly eyes on me. Okay, this is funny and they can laugh all they want. I think I've found my purpose in life. IT'S TO MAKE PEOPLE LAUGH WITH ME! Not at me though. I still hate The Cone.

I have to go back for more surgery, though I've been promised no Cone. Dr. P. says that because I probably had distemper, my adult teef are not there. I only have baby teef. Those baby teef don't want to come out and it's causing my mouth to be sore. Those suckers are coming out. I see more get-well squeakies in my future!

That surgery was much easier. But, now my tongue won't stay in my mouth. It hangs to the side. Hahahaha! I make a mess when I drink water. Ricky and Reno get yelled at when they play with the water bowl. After they are yelled at, I walk over and make a mess. Ha, make fun of me when I had to wear The Cone, will you? Then, I let my tongue get super wet from the water, and I go kiss Mom. She says I'm going to make a great kissing booth dog. Whatever that means!

All healed up. I feel so much better.

Chapter 10

2013 - Training Begins

I'm pretty excited! I'm going to begin my training as official Assistant Pet Tech Instructor #7. That means I help Mom train people to learn pet first aid so that they have the skills to save the life of their pets!!!!! Ricky is #4, and it's his job to make sure I know what to do. Boy, is he serious about it. I've already got a list of acceptable and not acceptable behavior from him. The problem is that all the fun stuff is on the not acceptable list. No poking butts, no rooting around in people's stuff they leave on the floor, no checking out what's going on in the hallways. Yeah yeah yeah. I've got to be me!

    Mom says it's a small class not too far from home, and it's a good place to get my feet wet. That's not all that got wet. Me and Ricky had to have a bath. Mom said no stinky dogs can be assistants. I'm not stinky, I'm like a fine wine that needs time to age! I was going to roll in some mud, but Mom said if I did I'd have to get another bath. I had to think on that. Mud/Bath, Mud/Bath. Mud/Bath. I'll get to that mud when I get home from work. That's right. I'm going to be an official working dog! You'd think Baby would be jealous, but he just snorted at us and called me a sucker.

    Spirit: What's a sucker? It must be something good. Probably has to do with my official working dog title.

    Ricky: Ignore him. He has no idea how great it is to travel with Mom. There's road food and people pet us and there's road food.

    Spirit: What's road food?

    Ricky: Ohh, it's spectacular! I can't even describe it. You'll have to experience it.

Dad: *Mary, Take a look at Ricky. He looks weird. He's drooling. I think his eyes are glazed over.*
Mom: *He's fine. He's over excited about teaching tomorrow.*

The night before, Mom started to load up the car with everything she needed to teach the pet first aid class. Took her quite some time especially with Ricky asking, are we leaving, over and over again. Ricky wouldn't even sleep in the bed with us. He wouldn't move from the door that goes to the car. Mom had to put a blanket down for him.

In the morning, Mom put me and Ricky in the car surrounded by the stuffed dogs. A lot of them. It was a little cramped, but we each had our own crate. Mom's friend, Beth, came to help us teach. I like Beth. She smells like other dogs.

Ricky: Sometimes Beth brings her dog. But, Annie doesn't follow the rules. She's always looking for food, and one time, she

2013 - Training Begins

2013 - Training Begins

escaped the class room and went over to the hotel's kitchen and the restaurant. She even tried to join a family eating their lunch. Can you imagine?

Spirit: I already like Annie. I hope to meet her one day!

Beth had treats for me and the bonus is she doesn't give me a bath. Me and Ricky get special bandanas. It's our work uniform. None of my other brothers have a uniform. Me and Ricky are special. I'll give Mom this one. I wouldn't want to get my special bandana dirty from the mud. Ricky says when we go to trade shows, the uniform is a babe magnet. All the Poodles love a man in a uniform.

It didn't take long to get to our working place. The first thing that Mom and Beth do is set up our crates in the room in case we get tired and need a place to relax. I'm not old like Ricky. I won't need it. Then she sprayed all of us, including Beth, with this stuff that smelled good. Ricky says it helps to keep us calm and focused.

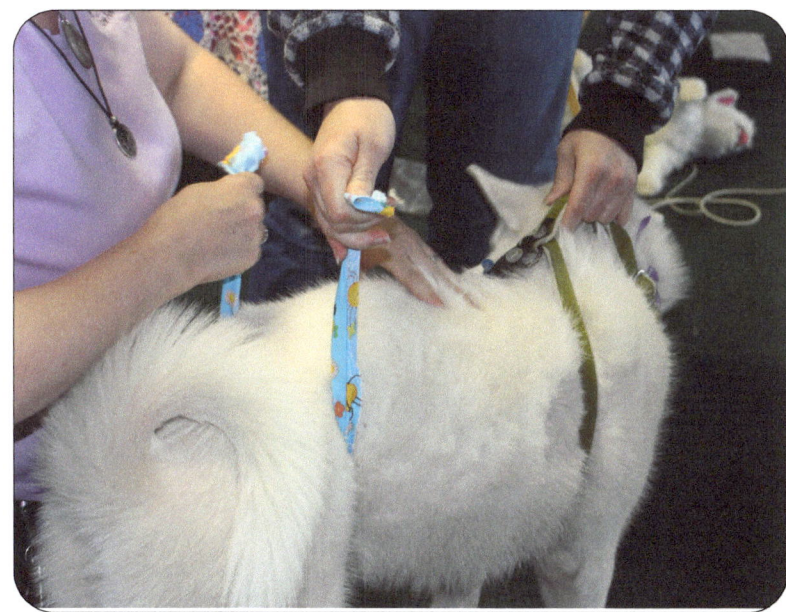

I got to greet everyone who came to the class. I was very professional. But Mom spoiled some fun for me. She told everyone that even though I was blind, my nose worked just fine and to not leave anything on the floor that they didn't want my nose in. I just have to assume that if they left something on the floor it was okay for me to check out. Hahaha! It's their bad if they didn't believe Mom.

I learned something new. People also like yummy snackies. One of the best parts of the class was when everyone came over to feel for a pulse. Mom said it was a skill that was like riding a bike. The more they did it and practiced, the easier it would be to find when they needed to have that information. I could feel the happy when they found my pulse. They would also kiss the top of the head. I love my job!

Whenever Ricky went into his crate to rest, I went into mine so he wouldn't feel left out. Not that I was tired or anything!

Ricky: Dude, you were exhausted. I went into my crate, so you'd follow.

Spirit: Ok Boomer, whatever you say. I was not tired. I was just giving Mom and Beth a chance to shine as they were teaching.

Ricky: When we got home, you slept all the way till the next morning.

Spirit: Mom said I did so well that I will be going to all the classes with you from now on.

Ricky: You still need some work. But you weren't as bad as I thought you'd be.

Chapter 11

2014 - One Sexy Beast

I'm told I'm one sexy beast. Rawrr! Whatever that means. I'm not sure being sexy is worth the time and effort it takes. But I am getting loads of kisses and everyone wants to take a picture with me. I think I might be a celebrity now. I mean the smoochies are great, but everyone wants a piece of me. I need an agent!

So, how did I become so sexy? Glad you asked!. My friend Kristin at the vet's office got a book on creative grooming that she would read to me. Not much of a story line, but Kristin seemed very excited about it and asked Mom if she could use me as a model. I definitely need an agent.

I spent the entire day in the tub!!!! What the hell?! Got all wet and then all sorts of creams were rubbed into my coat. I had to keep still. Only because I was curious did I allow this. I'm not sure there will be a repeat. All day, everyone walking past would remark on how colorful I was. Comments like "Boy Kristin, got enough colors there?" and, "He's kinda bright Kristin!" all day long. I wish I could see colors. Colors must be so wonderful. Kristin would have to stop and wait for everyone to take a picture. Hold up, people. Every time Kristin has to stop for a photo op, I have to spend more time in the tub. I'm going to have to ask Ricky if he has an agent. Kristin took me out of the tub and dried and fluffed me up. Kaeley came by and put a necklace on me and said I'm ready for Mardi Gras since I'm all purples, greens, and golds. As long as Mardi Gras has squeakies, I'm game!

I think the necklace was the finishing touch. Even Dr. P. was amazed. He kept saying Wow! I'm going to have to talk to Mom about getting me more of these necklaces.

I just heard Mom's car. She's here! Boy, won't she be surprised? Kristin said we were going to walk the red carpet just like they do at awards show when Mom came into the office. Yep, definitely need an agent! I know from the trade shows that awards are a big deal. Ricky told me there are prizes and stuff and people get very excited about them.

Turns out the red carpet was a bunch of towels laid on the floor. I have to assume they were all red towels. Mom squealed when she saw me. Just like my second Mom. I never heard her squeal before!

Mom thinks I'm beautiful. She told me I was a sexy beast. Dad remarked on how colorful I am. Everyone who can see colors, consider yourself lucky. Here I am, all these colors, and I can't appreciate how beautiful I am.

I wish I could see what color is. Ricky and Baby must be in awe of me. They've been just following me around.

Ricky: I can't believe what they did to you.
Baby: Hahahahaha!
Ricky: I can't believe what they did to you.
Baby: Hahahahaha!
Ricky: I can't believe what they did to you.
Baby: Hahahahaha!

They must be jealous of my sexiness. And, I found out that I'm going to go to a trade show with Ricky and Mom soon. I just need some more training.

Spirit: Hey Ricky, I hope these colors last until that trade show we're going to.
Ricky: I can't believe what they did to you.
Baby: Hahahahaha!
Spirit: Do you have an agent? I think I need one.
Ricky: I can't believe what they did to you.
Baby: Hahahahaha!

2014 - One Sexy Beast | **43**

Baby and Ricky are obviously blinded by my sexiness. I can't even hold a conversation with them right now.

I almost forgot! I have another job! This one is so much fun. Mom takes me to this place where there are a lot of really old people. They love my colorful self. They give lots of smoochies and hugs, and then we all sit around and Mom plays her singing bowls for them. Singing bowls are pretty cool. Mom packs them very carefully away from me. Hahaha! 'Parently, they are fragile and if I break one, it's going to cost me a year of squeakies. I know that there are four bowls because they all sound different. I feel so calm and sleepy when she plays them. Mom says we come here because many of the residents have trouble sleeping and the singing bowls help relax them so they can sleep better.

Chapter 12

Skunk Slayer

Who da man? I'm the man! Protecting my family from those dangerous skunks. Boy, do they smell bad!

My brothers were making fun of me because I'm all different colors. I told them they're just jealous and how I wished I could see how beautiful I was and that maybe they ought to appreciate their eyesight. But then, danger entered my yard and threatened my family! There I was out playing with my ball when I sensed something off to the right. My senses are amazing! I knew it didn't belong here. It was an intruder. Not the good kind of intruder that has squeakies and smoochies.

I was ferocious! Instinct took over and, before that skunk knew what happened, I had it in my mouth. Its defenses were pitiful. Smelly, but pitiful. I could hear my brothers yammering on in the background. Who's not listening to who right now?

Ricky: Mommommommommommom!

Mary: *Hey, Ricky, what's up? Oh shit! You stay put.*

I was so close to killing it and mounting it on my crate when Mom came screaming out and made my cheering section go inside. They didn't go willingly. Mom had to pick them both up. I could hear her grunting carrying Reno into the house. They're not making fun of me anymore now, are they? My jaw was a steel trap. She had to pry the skunk out of my mouth.

I have to go to the vet now because mom is worried about some little scratch on my face. Dad just came home as Mom was getting ready to put me in her car, but Dad said to take his car since it was outside. He's going to regret that decision. Boy, do I smell! Mom gave him clear instructions not to let the other dogs back out until he gets the skunk out of the backyard without causing it further harm.

Spirit: Hey You Skunk! Don't you come back here or maybe next time my Mom may not be able to save your life!

Mom: *Are you trying to get the skunk out of the yard with a sword?!*

Dad: *I'm not going to hurt it, just guiding it towards the gate.*

I couldn't tell if Mom sounded amazed at Dad or was impressed with Dad or just couldn't believe he was using a sword.

Mary's note: *Total disbelief. And sorry, I didn't have the presence of mind to video record it.*

It was quite breezy in the car driving to the 'mergency vet because Dr. P. was off today. I think Mom had all the windows open. I will say that this new vet was quite deferential to this warrior. As soon as we walked into the hospital, someone came running and said I'd be more comfortable waiting in the car rather than on the cold, hard floor and the vet would come out to see me. Mom told them not to make me wait too long or she'd have to bring me back inside. You tell 'em Mom. Don't make me wait! The vet came out pretty quickly, cleaned up the battle wounds and gave me two shots. Ouch!

As soon as I got back home, all the other dogs were deferential to me. They knew I'm da man of the house. Well, second-in-, wait no, third-in-command now. Ricky said he was proud of me. Even Marcus popped in to say he was impressed!

Marcus: Dude, I am so impressed. This was better than the time Ricky brought Mom a live bird. It was still wriggling and everything.

Ricky: I don't know what came over me. It flew right past me, and I went after it.

Marcus: It was delicious. Thank you!

Dad: *While you're out there giving Spirit a bath, roll up my windows. You left them all down.*
Spirit: Wait, what?
Mom: *Your car needs to air out.*
Dad: *He doesn't smell that bad.*
Spirit: Correct, I don't smell that bad.
Mom: *Whatever you say. Those little air freshener trees are not going to cut it. Come on Spirit, Let's go.*

Mom told me that the next day, Dad put 40 air freshener trees in his car. LOL maybe he should have listened to Mom!

The Victim! (Skunk's testimony):

What a day! First this Husky in colors I have never seen before tried to gum me to death. It had no teeth. What's up with that? He just kept swinging me back and forth and didn't even let go when I blasted him with urine. There were other dogs just cheering him on. "Go Spirit, go Spirit!" and "Someone get mom." I tried to get them in the urine blast, but they were too far away. Finally, some woman comes running and pries his mouth open, and I fall to the ground. I appreciate that she removed the other dogs first, but man does my neck hurt. I think I need a chiropractor. To top it all off, when I couldn't find the way out of the yard, this man with a sword kept poking me towards the exit. None of my friends or family believe me. You'd think, I'd have legendary status that I survived a Husky AND SWORD attack. But no, just laughter and asking if I got into that catnip garden again.

Mary's note: *I am so sorry there are no pictures.*

Chapter 13

Trade Show Road Trip

Woot woot! I'm going to my first trade show as an employee of Mom. (I wonder if I have to fill out a W9?)

Ricky has been teaching me stuff and it's the big-time, baby! I got this handled. Ricky's been telling me it's not like the classes I've helped with so far. Those were a short ride and not a lot of people. Move over old man. It's time for some young blood. We're going to Hotlanta for the Atlanta Pet Fair. Me and Ricky always know the night before a class because Mom packs up the car before we go to sleep. But who can sleep?! Ricky sleeps by the garage door. No sneaking out without Ricky being alerted!

Ricky has been giving me pointers. The most important one is something called "road food." I'm not sure what that is, but Ricky says not to eat what Mom normally feeds us. Hold out for the good stuff.

Oh boy, oh boy, oh boy! I have my own crate with a bed and my toys. Though I don't see why I have to stay in the crate. How can I look out the window and hear everything? There's trees and cows and horses and cars. The smells are amazing. Good thing I have my own seeing eye dog to put a name to a smell.

Spirit: What's that Ricky?
Ricky: A cow.
Spirit: What's that Ricky?
Ricky: A cow.
Spirit: What's…
Ricky: They're cows. There are a lot of cows. It's going to be cows forever.

Mary: *Hey, what are you doing?*
Spirit: Checking out the snacks in the bag.
Mary: *Beth, pull over, I have to put Houdini back in the crate.*
Beth: *Are you sure you're closing the door correctly? I'll lock him in this time.*

Haha! Mom's getting annoyed that she has to stop and put me back in my crate. Beth thinks she's smarter than me. I'll have to dispel her of that notion. Doesn't matter if the door is facing the wall. There's no containing this Husky!

Spirit: What's that Ricky?
Ricky: A horse. Before you continue, It's one horse and another thousand cows.
Beth: *Hey, what are you doing?*
Spirit: Checking out the snacks in the bag.
Mary: *Snort!*

It's such a long ride that we stopped for the night at a motel. It's my first time at a motel! Mom claimed the bed near the air conditioner. At first, me and Ricky slept with Mom, but Ricky is a bed hog and he went to sleep with Beth instead. Everybody was tired, something about taking longer than it should because someone kept getting out of the crate.

Ricky: I was not the bed hog, you were. Besides, I don't get to see Beth that often.
Spirit: Whatever Dude, I've got Mom all to myself!

They got us up early and Ricky would not eat brekkfus.

Ricky: Don't eat it.
Spirit: Why? I'm hungry.
Ricky: Didn't you notice we got hamburgers last night with bread and everything?

Spirit: Yeah.
Ricky: THAT'S ROAD FOOD! If you eat the brekkfus, then we won't get any more road food.
Spirit: Good to know.
Ricky: Mom will be back with scrambled eggs soon.
Spirit: OOH!

Why they call it Hotlanta, I don't know. It's freezing here! I'm thinking it should have been called Cold-lanta. This place is different from the motel we were at last night. They made us wait in the car last night and our room was right where we parked. This time I got to walk through a hotel and everyone stopped and petted me and Ricky. We're the toast of the town! We took the 'vator and it was fast. One minute the doors closed and then swoosh, the doors opened again and we were someplace else.
Ricky: Elevators are freaky. We're moving but not going anywhere. Just freaky.
Mom was under the impression I was staying in my crate while she left the hotel. Ha! Not happening, this is fun. No matter how she tries to keep me contained, I break free. As soon as I hear her opening the door, I run and sit on the floor so the first thing she sees is me not in my crate. Ricky was yelling at me about staying in the crate, and yammering on about rules and such. He earned the right to stay on the bed, yada yada yada. Whatever!
Tomorrow, I will earn my keep!. Mom's paying me in squeakies. Oooh, smell chicken. I hope dinner is served.

Ricky's note: *It was bad enough that he wouldn't stay in the crate while driving using some bullshit excuse that he had to see everything. He's blind!!! But he has to stay in his crate when we're in the hotel. Those are the rules. I don't because I earned the right to stay on the bed when Mom goes out. Spirit has not earned that privilege yet. I'm getting tired. I need to get this overconfident child up to speed. He needs some work, but I'm confident he'll be able to handle it. I remember when I thought I could take over the world. Everyone will love him as much as they love me.*

Trade Show Road Trip | 53

Chapter 14

Atlanta Pet Fair

Oh boy, oh boy, oh boy! Mom put my bandana on AND a special badge that tells everyone I'm one of the speakers. Neither me nor Ricky ate breakfast. Too excited! Mom is just going to have to bring snackies. I gotta pee.

Spirit: What the hell, Ricky? Why did you grab the leash and drag me to the 'vator?

Ricky: You said you had to pee. There will be no accidents on my watch! And during class you let Mom know if you have to pee or I will drag you to the door of the classroom. This is the big time. You will act professional. Got it?

Spirit: Yes sir!

If I had eyes, they'd be rolling around to the back of my head. He's so bossy. Mom took me and Ricky outside while Beth got breakfast. Boy, everyone knows Ricky. The security guards didn't even check his badge. They checked mine.

James: *And who is this?*

Mary: *James, meet Spirit. He's Assistant Pet Tech Instructor #7.*

James: *I see, first day on the job, Spirit?*

Spirit: Yes sir!!

James let us in the classroom that Mom and Beth had set up last night. I like James. He laughed when I gave him one of my wet, sloppy kisses. Our crates were already in the room with bowls of water. Mom closed the door and let me explore the room. It was bigger than any room we taught in before. So many tables and chairs. Beth came back and then Mom ran to get some breakfast.

Spirit: Why didn't Mom and Beth go together and leave us here to explore?

Ricky: Because they are not sure you won't get in trouble if they are both gone. There are cords and things with hard edges you're not familiar with yet. It won't take you long to find your way around.

And then the floodgates opened! People, lots of them, started walking in. Some of them came with other dogs. Some people said hi to Ricky (boy, he is famous! I wonder why he doesn't have an agent? I'll have to have a discussion with him). I made sure I greeted everyone and let them know I didn't get breakfast in case they had extra snackies on them. I made a mental note of whose bags had what snackies in them for later perusal. Perhaps when they weren't paying attention.

Ricky: Pace yourself or you'll get tired too quickly.

Spirit: Listen up old man, I've got this.

Ricky: Don't say I didn't warn you!

I heard the doors close and then Mom started to speak.

Mary: *If you've been to this class before, you all know Ricky then.*

I heard so many people say "Hi Ricky" all at the same time.

Mary: *I'd like to introduce you to Spirit. He's in training. You may have noticed that he is blind, but I assure you his nose works just fine. If you have anything in your bags that you think Spirit might be interested in, I'd suggest you put them on the table instead.*

Mom! Don't give away my secrets!

Hahaha! Fortunately for me, not everyone believed her. Everyone laughed when I found a bag on the floor and started to check out what they brought and someone yelled "Hey!" or "What Are You Doing There Mister!" What can I say, I'm curious!

The first day of class was amazing. And I'm told there are 2 more days of this. How'd I get so lucky? There were so many people. Many of which left goodies on the floor for me to find even though Mom tried to warn them. Haha! You snooze, you lose! I'm going to have to have a conversation with her regarding not telling them my secrets.

♡

Mom and Beth assumed I would be so tired that I wouldn't try to escape from the crate later in the evening when they went to dinner. She was wrong though. Even though I was tired, I figured out how to bypass her latest attempt to keep me contained and then slept on the floor until I heard them in the hallway, and then, I'd run to sit in front of the door as if I was there all the time. Ricky was so mad.

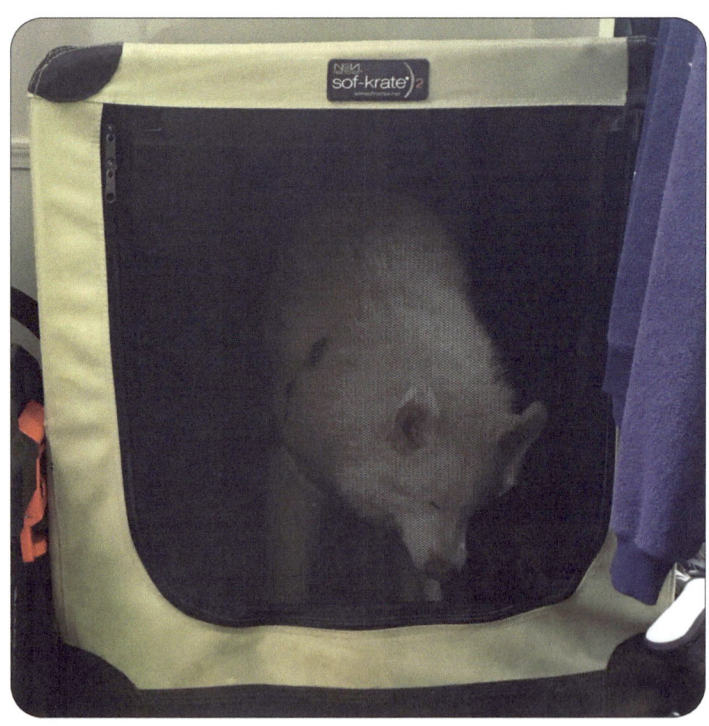

I was born for this. I can't wait to go to another trade show. I want to be as well known as Ricky. Everyone knew Ricky and called him by name. He even gave me pointers about how to talk to Poodles, and he introduced me to all his friends. Most of the Poodles were snooty and didn't want to talk to regular Joes like me and Ricky. I say screw them, but for some reason, Ricky just loved them even more. We played with some of the non-snooty Poodles, and I got to try so many different types of food. I love road food!

I may have slept the entire ride home. It was like a week!

Ricky: It was two days and I told you to pace yourself Youngblood. You missed all the cows.

Spirit: zzzzzzzzzz.

Chapter 15

I'm a Husky

On the way home from the Atlanta Pet Fair, Mom said we were going to make a pit stop at her friend Beatrice's house. Ricky likes Beatrice and told me all about the dogs that are there that we won't actually meet. Ricky says they are sled dogs and eat little dogs for fun. Does that mean they're made out of sleds? How would a sled eat a little dog? I thought they were Huskies like me. Ricky just sighed. When we got to Beatrice's house, they were in the yard. They were silent, and I could tell Ricky was a little nervous. I said hi as I was going up some steps.

Spirit: Hi guys, my name is Spirit!

Lana: I'm Lana, this is Hunter, and that's Windy. You should come play with us!

Spirit: Oh boy, I don't know why Ricky's so afraid of you. Do you look like sleds? I can't tell, I'm blind.

Lana: Come into the yard, and we'll tell you.

Ricky: Keep moving Spirit. They want to eat you.

Lana: Ricky, that's not nice. We won't eat him.

First off, I love Beatrice. She has all these kitties. I keep asking mom for a pet kitty, but so far I have been denied. I heard one of the kitties yell out "Husky in the House," and then I felt two of the kitties run past me like the wind and hide from me. Because I'm a Husky? I don't get it. But the third cat is fat and a little slower. His name is Peony.

Beatrice wouldn't let me see my Husky brother and sisters. She said they might consider me prey because I'm blind. Ha! We have a bond, and they can talk to me. She was mistaken. They just wanted to play with me.

Lana then said Beatrice might have a point, and that I had to stop acting like a Golden Retriever and more like a Husky. The Huskies discussed it amongst themselves and decided they were here to help. I've been lied to! I blame Ricky. He's my mentor, and I've been mimicking his behavior because I thought that was how I was supposed to act. I was so wrong! Fortunately, Lana got my priorities straightened out.

First off, they have been trying to catch Peony and eat him for a long time. If I was willing to grab Peony for them, they'd share their vast knowledge. I like kitties. So, I pretended to catch Peony as he was sitting on top of a grooming table. Beatrice was very excited about a new brush and was brushing Peony. I muscled my way in between Mom and Beth, and I managed to get a couple of hairs from his tail in my mouth. That was enough to convince my brethren to educate me on how to be a Husky as it was more than they were ever able to get. I tried to kiss Peony to apologize, but he was so mad at me and ran away. Not very fast mind you, as I was able to keep up with him.

Spirit: I just want to talk to you, Peony.

Peony: Go away you Husky.

Lana told me that baths are bad. That I should fight the whole process. The person giving the bath should be as wet as you are. It's only fair. I knew it! I knew it! I knew it! Here I was trying to be good. Good is for Golden Retrievers, not Huskies. We will see how the next bath goes, MOM. Though they did note that it never actually stopped the baths from happening, but they're willing to keep trying.

All of these things I learned over the course of a few short hours. I don't have to come inside just because my people want me to come in. I can come in when I'm Good And Ready.

Check!

And I had to dig escape holes. Lana told me about the time she started tunneling under the house but had to stop when water started filling in the hole. Lana was very impressed that I escaped from the crate while traveling and in the hotel. Told me to keep up the good work and maybe the next time I come, they won't try to eat me.

Oh crap, Ricky was right. These are some serious dogs. They aren't made out of sleds, they pull them. Why, I don't know. Where are they going with a sled? Are snackies involved? I can't see why I would pull a sled unless snackies were plentiful.

Finally, they taught me something called The Song Of My People. It's how we let all the other Huskies know that we are being forced to do something we don't want to and to sing in solidarity with them when we hear it. I can't wait to sing The Song Of My People the next time Mom tries to give me a bath.

Beatrice had lots of good food and told me to leave Peony alone. Mom was apologizing to Beatrice saying that I never went after cats before.

Mary: *I was thinking about getting a cat because he was so good with them.*

Beatrice: *He's a Husky. I wouldn't trust them around cats. Their prey drive kicks in.*

Spirit: That's right MOM! I'm a Husky. No wait, I want a pet cat. I won't eat it. I promise!

Dammit. All in all this was a real eye-opening weekend. I can't wait to come back and see Beatrice next year.

Chapter 16

Poke the Butt and My Stuff

Boy, Reno is a grump! He's one of my other brothers. I don't talk much about him because he's such a sour puss. He's blind like me, but he used to be able to see. I never hear the end of it. He walks so slowly so he doesn't bump into things. I get it, but he's making his blindness control his life. He has no fun. I bounce off of things all the time. Hahahaha, including him! He hates that. I get the safety speech from him. He's worse than Ricky with his set of rules. You can't do this! You can't do that! I've got to be me. It's fun to run and play with my squeakies and the big ball.

OMG! The Big Ball! Mom calls it a beach ball and boy, can that ball move when you smack it! The only problem is that it pops when I pounce on it. It's almost as much fun as my squeakies. Mom must know where they are kept because by the next day, I have another one. Smack, smack, smack, POP! I like the beach balls the best. Mom got me different types of balls and says these should last a while. They do, but they're boring. They don't move very fast when I smack them. Sometimes I smack the beach ball so hard, I can't find it right away. That's the best. I have to put my talents to the test. I always find it. I suspect Mom sometimes pushes the Big Ball away from me in an effort to make the ball last longer.

Ricky: Oh, she does.

Spirit: I knew it!

I don't let Ricky play with my squeakies because he destroys them to take the squeaky out. He can break his own toys, not mine. Reno can play with them, but I have to push it towards him because he can't see it. He's not using his nose very well. But, it makes

him happy to join in the play. Even Baby can play with them! Just not Ricky. All my squeakies are different. They feel and sound different. I have many squeakies. Now, whenever a squeaky has served its purpose, I leave it where Ricky can find it, so he will destroy it. Mom then feels bad for me and goes to get another squeaky out of the squeaky bag. The squeaky bag is magical. Mom sticks her hand in and comes out with a new squeaky!

There is a downside to squeakies. Sometimes Mom wants me to come in and I don't feel like it. I'm busy! There's animals on the other side of the fence I can smell. Though that skunk no longer comes by. I showed him who's boss. You stay on your side of the fence and I stay on mine, you skunk!

A couple of times, some people were hiding behind the fence doing stuff they weren't supposed to. I know that because I could hear them saying things like, did you get the beer, or hey that's supposed to be shared, and don't worry, they can't see us from the patio. I barked at them. Gotta pull my weight around here. They are up to no good. One time, they threw a bottle over the fence and it broke! I almost stepped on glass! Mom was mad, and she yelled at the neighbor lady. Neighbor lady said her kids would never drink beer and throw the bottle over the fence. Yeah right, neighbor lady.

I'll pretend I can't hear Mom or take a page out of Reno's book and act like I'm trying, but I can't see where I'm going and I'm lost. Then she squeaks one of my squeakies. I try to resist, but it's too much. I need the squeaky! And if I'm successful in resisting, she tells me she's going to give it to Ricky. That gets me running inside! Lana would be so disappointed in me. I hope she doesn't take my Husky Card away.

Ricky: Hahaha, yes, give me the squeaky! I destroyed my last one and need a new one.

Another game I like to play is what Mom calls Poke The Butt. That's where I poke my nose in someone's butt and then turn around like I have no idea who poked their butt. Couldn't be me! Everybody but Reno thinks it's fun as well. Well, Baby doesn't like it either. He bit me once. It hurt! And Mom got mad at him, but Baby didn't care. The upside is that I got a new Squeaky.

Baby: That's right. Poke my butt and you will get bit. There are no negotiations regarding this.

Spirit: Hahaha! Unless I want a new squeaky and am willing to take that risk.

I will goose anyone that I walk past. I always know where the butt is. It's that superior nose of mine! I can make everyone laugh and piss Reno off at the same time. I will play Poke The Butt anywhere, anytime. At the vet's office, at tradeshows, at home. It doesn't matter. If you have a butt, I'm gonna poke it! The best part of Poke The Butt is all the smoochies I get afterwards. Even Ricky thinks it's funny. Everyone but Reno and Baby like the game. Well, and a couple of sourpusses at a trade show didn't think it was funny. I didn't get any smoochies from them. The most fun I had with Poke The Butt was coming up behind Mom or Dad after they got out of the shower. My cold wet nose on a naked butt is the best!

Baby: Okay, that was pretty funny.

Chapter 17

The Smurf

Sometimes, Mom and Dad go someplace without us. The nerve of them, right? I didn't know that there are some places that don't allow dogs. I don't want to go there anyway. Pfft. I bet it's no fun. I'd rather be somewhere I'm appreciated! Me and my brothers go to the vet and stay with them instead. They love us there, not like those other boring places. Me especially, I get to hang out with my ladies. Ooh yeah! I have a bed right by the reception counter and hang out while they do vet stuff. The best part is I get to play with the "office kitties" again. They miss me. I have to talk to Mom again about getting my own pet kitty.

When Mom dropped me off, she and Kristin were talking. OMG they can talk! Just go already, I have kitties to play with. Anyway, Kristin asked Mom if she could dye me again, since I did so well the first time. I did so well, Kristin, because I didn't know what was involved and how long it would take and that it would involve a bath. My new Husky brethren told me that real Huskies don't need baths and I need to make that clear. But, I was still new with Mom at the time, and I was hedging my bets.

Mom told Kristin not to do something so involved, It took too long to fade out.

Thank you, Mom.

"But since it's close to the 4th of July, maybe some red ears and a blue tail to go along with his white fur.

Mommmmm!

Kristin was so excited to get started, she didn't even give me a chance to play with the kitties. Right into the tub! I need to put a stop to this. I'm already getting too many baths at home. I knew I had my opening when Kristin told me she only had enough red dye to do my ears. All I will say is that Lana and Windy would be so proud of me. I let out a mournful howl and Kristin spilled the red dye on my back. Hahaha! No more red dye, Kristin.

Then she said that she had plenty of blue dye, and she'll figure out how to fix the red splotches later. You HAD plenty of blue dye, Kristin. Muah ha ha! You HAD plenty of blue dye.

I jumped up to give her a kiss and she knocked the blue dye all over me! She screamed and everyone came running. There were a couple of What The Fucks, followed by laughter, and a might as well dye him entirely blue as he's 75% blue anyway.

So, now I'm all blue, and everyone is calling me Papa Smurf. Papa Smurf must be famous, and I bet he has an agent. If only I could read the Yellow Pages!

Apparently, I've made Kristin very upset. She is now worried that Mom will be mad at her and that she's a complete failure as a creative groomer. I momentarily felt bad until I 'membered that this involves a bath. Sometimes you just have to be cruel to be kind. Hahaha! Kind to me that is. They took me outside to take a picture to send to Mom to prepare her for my gloriousness. Bet she won't ask Kristin to dye me again!

While Kristin took me outside for the photo shoot, this lady walks up and tells me how beautiful I am and how she's never seen a bright blue dog before. What breed am I, and who is my breeder?

I have never known Kristin to be silent. Am I the only Husky that is bright blue? Wait. AM I THE ONLY BRIGHT BLUE DOG IN THE WORLD!?! I definitely need an agent now. Anyway, Kristin told her that I was a white Husky that she dyed blue. Then, the lady got all annoyed with Kristin about how cruel it is to dye dogs an unnatural color.

And while I agreed that baths are cruel, she needed to chill out as I AM THE ONLY

The Smurf | 67

The Smurf

BRIGHT BLUE DOG IN THE WORLD!!! I woofed at her. Don't be making my friends upset! Glad she's not my Mom.

During the day, I get to stay at the reception area. In the evening, I get kenneled with my brothers. They are so jealous of me.

Baby: WTF did they do to you now? You're all blue.

Ricky: *Sigh*

Spirit: I know. Kristin was trying for red ears and a blue tail. I'm getting tired of all these baths, and I jumped and knocked the dye out of her hand, and it spilled all over me. I bet Mom won't want to dye me anymore.

Baby: I'm thinking you don't know Mom well enough! Though I'm impressed with the effort.

We all knew the day Mom and Dad were coming to pick us up because Kristin was all upset and saying that Mom was going to be mad at her. Everyone was comforting her. Not me. Make your bed and go lie in it. Mom was never going to ask her to dye me again.

Mary's note: *That was where he was wrong. I thought it was the funniest thing I ever saw. It was not the*

Playing with friends at the vet's office.

last time we colored him either. And the creative groomers at the trade shows used him as a model, which he loved!

Spirit's rebuttal: *The creative groomers at trade shows don't give me a bath and they give me a platform to show off my beautifulness. There is lots of hugging and pictures taken. I am in wedding pictures, MOM! I have to talk to Angela and Lori, my favorite creative groomers, about getting an agent. They're famous. I bet they have one.*

But all Mom did was laugh and told Kristin she did a great job considering I was a Husky and that most creative groomers work on Poodles, so not to beat herself up.

MOMMMMM!

Chapter 18

2016 - It's a Bad Day

OMG Ricky just collapsed and can't get up! Dad is all freaked out and called Mom to come home. Everything will be fine when Mom comes home.

Spirit: What's the matter Ricky?

Ricky: I don't know. I don't feel good. I'm so tired, and I can't get up.

Spirit: Don't worry! Dad called Mom, and she's on the way home. She'll know what to do!

As soon as Mom came home, they picked up Ricky and went down to the vet. Dr. P. will get him fixed up in no time.

Marcus: Listen up, guys. This is not good. Ricky doesn't have much time left in his physical form. It's time for him to join me and Kira. It'll be scary for him, and you'll need to be strong for him and mom and dad.

Spirit: No no no! NO! He can't leave us. I'm not finished with my training.

Marcus: He will still be here for you, just not in a physical form.

Baby: I'll help you Spirit. I've been through this a couple of times. It's close for me as well.

Spirit: Wait, what? No no no!

Mom and Dad and Ricky came home a couple of hours later to confirm what Marcus said. Dr. P. and a heart specialist can't do anything.

Spirit: I don't want you to go. You can't go yet!

Ricky: I don't want to go either. But I have to. Mom will not let me suffer. I'll still be here for you. Your training is complete. You will be fine. Make sure the Poodles don't forget me when you're at a trade show. Listen to Mom!

Spirit: I love you.

I don't want to talk anymore. It's a bad, bad day. Ricky, my brother, my mentor, my friend, just died. He had a hemosarcoonaganioan. Everyone in my home is shocked and crying. Even Reno. We had just got back from the Atlanta Pet Fair and Ricky fell down. He was fine and then he wasn't. I'm told the cancer was too fast, and it spread too quickly. Mom stayed home with Ricky, and sometimes, she had to take him to the vet to drain the fluid around his heart until one day she came home without him. He was here one day, and now he's not. I don't want to talk about it.

Mary's note: Ricky had a Hemangiosarcoma, an aggressive form of cancer on his heart. Two weeks from diagnosis to loss. He had had a cancer screening six months prior with a clean bill of health.

It wasn't long before Baby left us too. Dad was a wreck. Now it's me, just me and Reno. I don't even feel like poking his butt.

Chapter 19

Real Friends

What is it with Poodles? I don't get why Ricky was so enamored of them. I think Ricky imagined he was Billy Joel and he'd get his *Uptown Girl*, but the truth of the matter is they don't appreciate the average Joe. Not that I'm an average Joe. I'm pretty special, but obviously can't tell them how beautiful they are. I see their inner souls. At a trade show, it's all about, don't touch me you'll mess up my hair, or check out my nails, and did you see that collar on Bella, so not her color!

Marcus was right, Ricky came with us to the trade shows in his not physical form. Would you believe he was still trying to talk to the Poodles?

Ricky: Go introduce yourself to that Poodle. She's cute!

Spirit: I'm going to go poke her butt is what I'm going to do.

Ricky: Does anyone miss me?

Spirit: Everyone who matters is missing you. Mom is getting lots of hugs. Pearl misses you.

Ricky: Don't poke her butt.

Spirit: I would never. Hahaha! Yeah, I will.

Not all the Poodles are stuck up. First there's Falcor. Me and Falcor are friends. She doesn't mind getting her hair mussed while playing with me. Falcor is like, my mom, Lori, will fix it anyway. I like Lori too. She and Mom talk and talk and talk. Which is okay, because that's more me and Falcor time.

Lori and her friend, Angela, are creative groomers, and they use me as a demo dog in their classes. One time, they put googly eyes and drew on eyebrows and a mustache on me. Everyone laughed and petted me. Not only did all the groomers take my photo, but I'm in gazillion wedding photos thanks to not only those googly eyes, but all of Kristin's dye jobs before a trade show. I'll have to think about cutting Kristin some slack. Thinking, thinking, thinking. I have to stay true to myself. So, probably not!

But also there was Pearl. Pearl was famous! She was a Creative Grooming Competition Dog! She won contests! I blame her for giving Ricky the wrong impression about Poodles. She was always nice and would play with us. She missed Ricky. Pearl's mom is Dawn Omboy. I love it when Mom spends time talking with people. I bet Pearl has an agent.

The most fun was when Lori and Angela prepped me for the Kissing Booth for a fundraiser. Let me tell you how many people paid to kiss me. I raised a lot of money that day. That reminds me, I have to speak to Lori and Angela about an agent. I mean I always get paid in squeakies, but am I getting enough squeakies?

I'm pretty famous, and you'd think those Poodles would appreciate that, but noooooo. I'm more famous than my Mom. The security guards at the show recognize me right away, and I don't have to show my badge, but my Mom does. I bet those Poodles have to show some ID before they are allowed in.

Me and Angela.

Real Friends

My other good friend at the trade shows is Jazzy. She, of course, is not a Poodle, but is always at a booth with her mom, and we get to play. I have so many trade show friends who are not Poodles. Delise is another. She's not a dog at all, but a human who is always at the shows. I beta test some of her bows by walking around the show floor with her latest creation. She tells me I'm the best Brand Ambassador. And then there's Cutter. Me and Cutter were roommates at the New England Grooming Show. He borrowed my tie for professional headshots. I bet he has an agent. His mom didn't bring any cheese for him, but I'm a good roommate and snuck him some when his mom wasn't looking.

Cutter: Cheeeesssseee!

The best part of going to trade shows is when I make people cry. Not sad crying, but happy crying. One time a woman just hugged me and started crying. Her husband told my Mom that their dog just went blind. They were unsure about his quality of life and were thinking about letting him go. Let him go where? I don't know. But after seeing me at the trade show having fun, they knew their dog would be okay. The husband said, it was watching me poke the butts that tipped the scales. Those Poodles hate poke the butt. Hahaha!

Another happy crying was when this little girl was hugging me. I was squooshed. I was all duded up as a Mardi Gras dog. Mom even put a bead necklace on me. Her mom was crying because the little girl was terrified of dogs. It was the first time she didn't run screaming away from a dog. I was in so many wedding photos that particular weekend.

Betcha Poodles don't do that!

I don't just have trade show friends. I have friends where I live as well. I have friends I hike with, and my best friend is Gracie. Gracie is one of Mom's clients. Mom is a mobile dog groomer who likes to spread the misery by giving other dogs a bath. Mom brings me with her when she goes to Gracie's house. We play in the yard, and then Mom takes Gracie to her van. For some reason, Gracie does not think this is torture, but she's a Labrador Retriever and not a Husky like me. Apparently, Labs LIKE water. I don't get it!

Gracie has a lot of toys. I mean LOTS of toys. Guess who gets to play with them while someone is getting a bath. That's right. Me! Personally, I think I'm getting the better end of this deal.

Gracie: You can play with my toys because I'm getting this great bath. I don't understand why you don't love this. I get massaged and brushed and she lets me kiss her.

Spirit: Yeah, I don't get it. See you in a couple of weeks!

Me and Gracie.

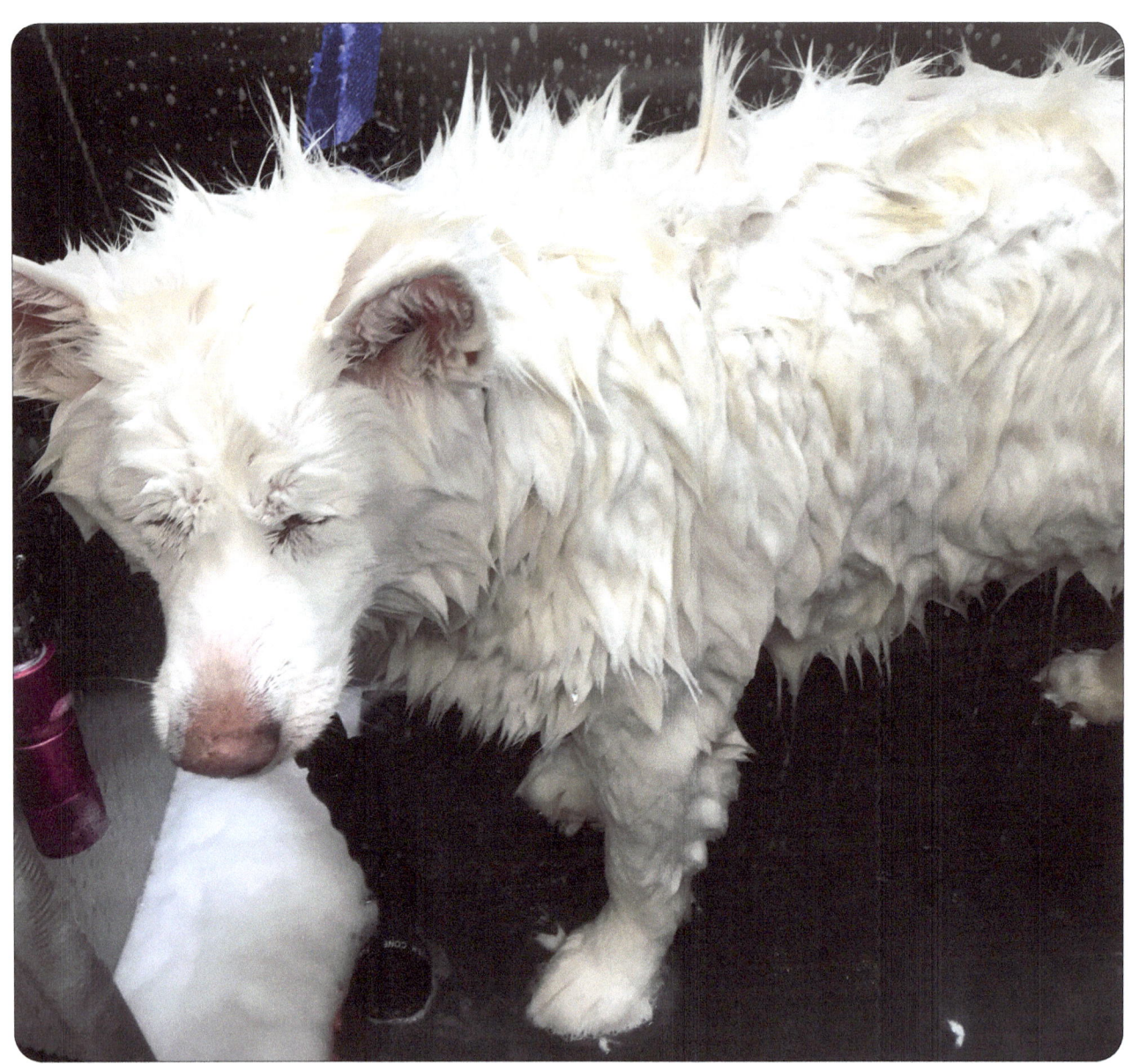

Chapter 20

Things I Dislike About Traveling to Classes and Trade Shows

Going to trade shows is not all fun and games.

First off is the bath. Why is it my problem that people don't appreciate the finer nuances of odor? You can tell so much about someone by their smells. I know what you had for breakfast, who you were talking to, what kind of cigarette you were just smoking (does your mother know?), and probably a couple of things you would rather I didn't mention!

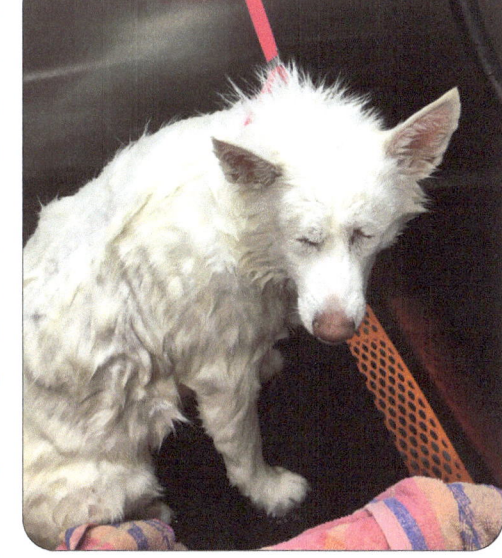

But, I'm the one who has to have a bath before going to a class or trade show. I'm wet. It takes forever to get dry. It's not like the twenty minutes Mom takes for a shower. It's hours and hours, maybe even a whole day!

All the dogs who go to a trade show get baths. Some of them have to take a bath before they leave and then again while they're at the show. Gasp! I would feel sorry for the Poodles if they weren't such assholes to Ricky.

Mary: *It's an hour and a half of your time to take a bath.*

Spirit: I beg to differ. In dog time, it's like ten hours.

Those baths wipe out our communication short cuts man! Kinda like we took away your cell phone's ability to text and use acronyms. Can't tell if a chick might like me without me getting all up in her business. I can see why Poodles are so snooty. Boundaries are gone.

The second thing is the long drive in a crate. How am I supposed to engage in conversation with my road tripping friends if I'm all the way in the back? Then, they get all annoyed when I get out of the crate. I don't know why they are all surprised when I do. I'm a Husky—'nuff said! I'm told it's unsafe, I could get hurt, yada yada yada! Back in the crate I go. Until I get bored anyways.

Then the food is crap. I mean, Mom got me this gross hamburger one time. They actually expect me to eat my home food. I'm not having any of that. They go out, I go out!

Mary: *That gross hamburger cost me $28.*

Spirit: Hey, aren't you supposed to just be checking spelling?

Mary: *Nope. I'm also your fact checker.*

Also, Beth hogs the bed. Beth is Mom's friend who teaches with her, so they travel together. I like to sleep with Beth, I can always sleep with Mom at home. But Beth doesn't like the cold, so I have to sleep with her so she gets all warm and wants to turn the AC on.

Beth: *I beg to differ on who hogs the bed, mister! I get up in the morning with leg cramps.*

Spirit: You're not drinking enough water. Not my fault. And who gave access to Beth to edit? MOM!

I know that Beth loves me though, because she once asked Mom if they should leave a light on for me when they went out. Me and Mom laughed at that one. Yes, Beth, leave a light on so the blind Husky can see where he's going!

Beth: *I love you my little dude.*

The one hotel Mom always complained about was the one I liked the best. The slider door to the outside was broken and wouldn't close all the way. That cool New England

Things I Dislike About Traveling to Classes and Trade Shows

air kept that room around the temperature of a refrigerator. I was in heaven! Mom said the only good thing about the door being broken was that there was no mold, and it was too cold for bedbugs.

And then, they leave me in the hotel room by myself. The nerve of them! At least they stopped trying to crate me and leave me on the bed with the AC on high. I can live with that. Although it was kind of fun to outsmart Mom and Beth. She called Beatrice one time asking for advice about keeping me in my crate. I could hear her laughing when Mom told her about my soft sided crate. That's right Beatrice, you tell her there's no containing this Husky! And then Beatrice told Mom the only crate that'll hold a Husky is an impact crate.

Hey! Beatrice! Don't be giving Mom any ideas!

Trade shows are also very loud. Hurts my ears. Sometimes I get turned around because sound seems to come from all directions. AND then, there are all the smells! Shampoo and conditioners and people wearing way too much perfume. Don't tell Mom, but sometimes it's nice to stay in the hotel room all by myself where it's quiet and the AC is turned on full blast for me.

Mary: *You know, if it's too much for you, you can stay home the next trip.*

Spirit: I'm filing some grievances. Me and Falcor and Jazzy AND a bunch of the snooty poodles are forming a union. Dad has told me all about them.

Mary: *Excuse me?*

Spirit: Yes. Dad says we should form a union. We have demands.

Mary: *Such as?*

Spirit: Number 1) No baths before the show. 2) No crates in the car. 3) One bag of shredded cheese each day. 4) Three new squeakies!

Mary: *And everyone in your union has agreed to this?*

Spirit: Yes! I'm the union delegate.

Mary: *How about one extra bag of cheese for the entire trip and one extra squeaky?*

Spirit: Deal!

Mary: *Don't you have to have your union vote on this?*

Spirit: Pfft! Those losers are on their own. They were mean to Ricky.

Chapter 21

I'm Annoyed

Well, I just found out that I can't go to Superzoo because, apparently, Las Vegas is too hot. The airplane is too hot. It's not safe. Yada yada yada! I think I'm quite capable of determining what risks I'm willing to take. I'm not buying the "it's too hot" argument. Let's start with the plane. Me going into the cargo hold was never an option anyway. I'll sit next to you on the plane.

Mary: *Yeah, no. It's not comfortable, you're going to be whiny. You can't walk up and down the aisle. And it's a long flight. You won't be able to go to the bathroom.*

Spirit: They have to make accommodations for me as you're my service person.

Mary: *Yeah, no. You have that backwards. The airline makes accommodations for people who need service dogs, not the other way around.*

Spirit: Can't you pretend I'm a service dog?

Mary: *Yeah, no. That makes it harder for people who need service dogs when those that don't try and take advantage of that loophole. There are people who need service dogs for mobility, or to detect an upcoming seizure or other medical event, to offer comfort for debilitating PTSD, or perform other medically necessary tasks.*

Spirit: Okay, then let's drive to Vegas!

Mary: *Yeah, no. You already complain about the sixteen-hour and two-day drive to Atlanta for the Atlanta Pet Fair. To drive to Las Vegas is 40 hours and five days.*

Spirit: I'll be good. I promise!

Mary: *You always promise, but an hour into the drive, you've escaped at least once and have* *started registering complaints that I have to listen to for the next 15 hours. I'm not doing that for 40 hours.*

Spirit: Let's table that discussion for the moment. Now your second issue is that Las Vegas is too hot for me. I've been in hotels before, the AC works well. I bet those casinos want to keep people inside and the inside is kept nice and comfortable.

Mary: *Yes they do, however, it's too much walking for you. This isn't your typical trade show that has about an hour of walking. It's a half hour just to get from the hotel to the trade show and then, hours of walking. It's exhausting. And you don't like the stroller.*

Spirit: The stroller is for babies. Pfft! I'm registering my complaints.

Mary: *Your "union" demands have already been met.*

Spirit: Well! I've got more complaints. The house is hot.

Mary: *Seriously? You're complaining about warm temperatures and think Vegas is going to be fine. You have two personal fans and your own portable AC unit. And if it's so hot, why did you smack the vents closed on the AC last night?*

Reno: Tell him Mom! The house is so cold I have to wear a sweater.

Mary: *We're all wearing sweaters in July.*

Spirit: Because I wasn't hot last night! But now I'm soooo hot.

Mary: *I see you. Don't you dare splash your paws in the water bowl and make a mess.*

Spirit: I'm hot and I pay attention in class and know how to cool myself down. Dipping my paws in the cold water. Hahaha!

The other complaint I have is that I have no one to play with at home anymore.

Reno: Hey! What about me?

Spirit: You complain about everything. I move too fast. You can't find the toy. Complain, complain, complain.

Mary: *Ahem!*

Spirit: Me and Reno are having a private conversation, MOM!

Spirit to Reno: Did you know that there are two puppies up for adoption at the vet? They were born there. Now the plan is if I can get those two puppies here, then I won't have to bother you. Imagine, no more poking the butt, or running into you, or any of the things I do to get you to play with me.

Reno: I'm listening. I'm sure Mom and Dad are aware.

Spirit: But, Mom says she doesn't want any more puppies. Something about a certain puppy ruining it forever. I bet she's talking about me. No other puppy can reach the bar I've set.

Reno: Yeah, I'm sure that's the reason.

Spirit: Anyway, Dad told me all about collective bargaining. You ask for more than you want and then you "settle" for a concession. So, I'm going to bug Mom about Vegas, but I'll let it go if she brings me those two puppies. She won't get me a cat.

Reno: What do I do?

Spirit: Just what you normally do. Tell Mom how much I bug you. Repeatedly. Maybe snap at me a couple of times! Just be sure to not actually bite me. Kira and Marcus are already mucking up anyone else's chances of adopting them. Kira says they belong here. Deal?

Reno: Deal!

Hey Mom, we haven't finished our conversation about Vegas.

Chapter 22

Hiking Off Leash

IT WAS AMAZING TODAY!

Mom let me hike without being attached to her today. For the first time, I felt like I was part of the hiking pack with my friends Socs, Lucy, and Winston. Socs is a Newfoundland, and he always waits for me. Lucy is a Labrador Retriever, and she says she tolerates me. I love her. And then there's Winston. Winston is one crazy guy. He runs through the woods like a mad dog. He can see the trees way before he gets close enough to run into them. They always got to run through the woods and play in the stream. AND TODAY, SO DID I! I love walking in the woods, even when I had to stay close to Mom so I wouldn't get hurt.

We hike every week. Just me and Mom. Reno does not want to come. We meet the guys at the entrance to a path that is behind one of Mom's favorite stores in Sherman, Connecticut called Happy Rainbows. She buys all sorts of rocks to bring home. I don't know why she buys them when there are so many rocks on the ground when we hike.

Mary: *Why do you pick one squeaky over the other? Or insist on new squeakies when there are so many at home?*

Spirit: Because I need all the squeakies. Ohhhhh!

As soon as we get there, Mom sprays me with this gross stuff to keep ticks off of me. Ticks are blood sucking parasites that pass disease onto unsuspecting good boys like me. Take that, you tick!

It all started when Donna, who lives with Socs, Lucy, and Winston, told Mom that we had been hiking long enough, and let's see how I do off leash. AND MOM SAID YES!

I know all the smells and how many steps over the bridge, where all the rocks that are sticking out of the ground, and especially where all the ouchie bushes are. I hate the ouchie bushes. Anyway. When Donna let her dogs go off leash, Mom took my leash off as well.

We all ran down the hill (40 steps) and over the slippy wood bridge (15 steps). I didn't run over the bridge because it was slippy. If I fell in the water, Mom would put the leash back on. That would suck! So, I was real careful over the bridge.

We all waited for Mom and Donna to catch up because we were coming up to a spot with all the big rocks that smell like pot and beer (35 steps), and sometimes there's broken glass here. I know the smell well because of the neighbor kids who smell the same. Winston used to run around the big rocks until he got glass in his paw. We all had to go home early that day because Winston got hurt. We were all mad at Winston, so now he waits. We waited and waited and waited until Mom and Donna picked up the broken glass. Come on, Mom, I want to run! Then we all ran up to where the stream is (150 steps). And Socs and Lucy said we had to wait until the moms catch up so we can go play in the stream. Except for Winston. He has the zoomies. He runs all over the place and somehow manages to be waiting with the rest of us when Mom and Donna catch up. I always knew the stream was there because I could hear the water. It's a very bubbly sound.

Boy, they're slow! They'd be faster if they weren't talking so much. Eventually, they came, and we all got to play in the stream (25 steps). I got all wet, and the water was so cold, but I loved it. This water is way better than the water in the tub when I get a bath.

Mary: *So all I have to do is make the water ice cold for you in the tub?*
Spirit: No, you have to remove the soap as well. Streams have no shampoo.
Mary: *What do you think is making the bubbly sound?*
Spirit: No, that's the sound of water gently cascading over the rocks. Don't try to fool me!

Don't tell Mom but when it was time to go home, I was so tired, so I stuck close to her. After the stream, we continue on the path until it comes to the big rocks from a different direction. There are lots of turns, and if I was off leash I wouldn't know when to turn. I can't wait to do this again next week. When we got back to the car to go home, Mom made sure there were no ticks on me. If she finds one, she squishes it with a rock. Take that, you tick!

Then we go to "talk" to Barrie which is code for "let's check out the new rocks." Her store always smells nice.

Winston, Lucy, and Socs have to wait in the car, but not me. Barrie likes me and lets me "talk" to her as well. Though that's code for "whose butt can I poke." Hahaha!

Chapter 23

2018 - My Brothers

Our plan worked, but I think there was a hiccup because Mom just came home with about a dozen small dogs. They tell me it's just two and their names are Speedy G and Cecil. I'm not quite sure that number is accurate. They're six months old and came from where Mom got me. I think this vet has my Mom's number and packed the suitcase with extra dogs. Anyway, I met them before when I was visiting the vet, and there were only two, but no one wanted to adopt them, so Mom brought them home. Mom calls them the Chiweenie Brothers. They're Dachshund, Miniature Pinscher, and Chihuahua. They were born at the vet's office, and their mom was adopted by Kristin.

Me and Cecil chilling out.

I don't really mind as they play and run with me, but they're so fast! I'm dizzy and can't help but wonder if they did sneak in a couple of extra dogs. Reno never wants to play. Cecil and Speedy are pretty careful not to run into him. I like Cecil a lot. He sleeps with me and leaves my squeaky alone. Speedy G is very dramatic. He's always screaming because he thinks it might hurt. Not that it does. The first time he screamed it freaked out of all of us. Mom especially 'cause she called the vet and asked

Playing with Cecil and Pooh.

point blank why didn't they tell her that Speedy is a Drama Queen; she nearly had a heart attack because she thought she broke him.

Speedy G: I think it's going to hurt, so I prep myself for the pain.

Spirit: Has it ever hurt?

Speedy G: No, but it doesn't hurt to be prepared.

Reno: Ah, a dog after my own heart!

I'm really glad the TWO dogs are here. We all sleep together. Even Reno cuddles up with us.

Reno: I have to talk to you.

Spirit: What's up?

Reno: It's time.

Spirit: Time for what?

Reno: It's time for me to cross over. My first mom has been waiting for a while and will help me cross over. I just wanted to let you know that I really didn't mind you poking my butt. I'm going to miss you and Mom and Dad. I'm so grateful that they provided me with a home as good as my first one.

Spirit: Excuse me?

Reno: I just wanted to wait until Cecil and Speedy G were here so you wouldn't be lonely.

Marcus: It'll be okay. Ricky and Akira are here as well and will assist.

Spirit: This is bullshit! So far, I have lost two moms, one sister, and four brothers. Hey you two, get over here.

Cecil/Speedy G: Yes sir!

Spirit: I'm about done with my family passing on. You two will not pass on while I am still around. Got it?

Cecil/Speedy G: Yes sir!

Shortly after Reno passed, I got another brother. Dad brought home Pooh Bear, whose first name was Taco. He immediately claimed Mom and said Mom is his. Dad thinks this is funny. At first I felt bad for him because I know what it's like to be passed around from place to place and be sick. He was in a truck too that came from Texas. Dad's sister got him for their mother who didn't want him. Said he was ugly, but I think it was the grief talking. Her dog, Junior, just passed as well. Sometimes, Junior would come and stay with us for a couple of weeks. Mom called it Summer Camp as he was a city dog. Ricky was scared of him.

Ricky: I wasn't scared of him, he claimed me as his pet. He was annoying.

Yeah, Ricky would run into his crate and beg to have Mom lock him in.

Pooh Bear: Back to me. We can all agree that Taco is a stupid name.

Dad wanted to call him Mugsy. What is it with Dad and dumb names? I think that's why Pooh Bear gives him so much crap.

Dad thinks he's so funny.

Pooh Bear: He's an asshole. I don't care for the way he looks at my Mom.

Mom calls Pooh Bear the chaperone. He always sits between Mom and Dad and barks at Dad. Dad just grabs Mom and kisses her, and then picks up Pooh Bear and kisses him.

Pooh Bear: Asshole.

Then Pooh claimed all my squeakies, and now all bets are off!

Pooh Bear: You can't possibly play with all the squeakies at the same time. So this one and this one, and also this one are now mine.

Spirit: MOM!

Mary: *Be nice and share.*

Pooh Bear: Yeah don't be an asshole. Hahaha!

Pooh Bear has decided he is going to live in Mom's sweatshirt.

Pooh Bear: That's right. This way I'm always close to Mom.

Mary: *I have such mixed feelings on this. On one hand, it's really cute, but then Dad comes in the room and Pooh literally bursts out of my sweatshirt to bark and growl at him. It's like a scene from 'Aliens.'*

Pooh Bear: Then maybe he should stay away.

Ernesto: *Come give me a kiss, Pooh Bear.*

Pooh Bear: Asshole.

Pooh Bear gets so annoyed when I go to trade shows and teach with Mom and come home with a new squeaky. I make sure to tell him all the things me and Mom did TOGETHER. Hahaha! Steal my squeakies, will you? The good thing about Pooh though is he is a cuddler too. We all sleep together in one giant bed. That is until Mom comes into the room and Pooh sits with her instead.

Brothers!

Chapter 24

2019 - Moving Across the Country

For a while I've been told about this place we're moving to. I don't know why we need to move, this place suits me just fine. I have my friends, all my squeakies are here, I know where everything is, especially the trees in the backyard. Apparently, Mom has had enough of the snow.

Spirit: Hey Mom, snow is the best part about living here. I love the snow!

Mary: *Yeah, well you don't have to drive in it, or shovel the mountains of snow off the deck so that you can walk down the stairs to the backyard. You get to just play in it. It still snows in the pacific northwest, just not a lot of it.*

Spirit: I'm registering my complaint. What about my squeakies and my bed? I'll miss my friends!

Mary: *All your stuff will be packed and moved. You'll still have your friends at the trade shows and you'll make new friends.*

Spirit: You two, get over here.

Cecil/Speedy G: Yes sir!

Spirit: Tell Mom you want to stay here.

Cecil/Speedy G: Mom, we want to stay here!

Spirit: You can go.

Cecil/Speedy G: Yes sir!

Spirit: See, they don't want to move either!

Mary: *Unfortunately, it's a done deal. The house is almost ready to move into.*

It's been crazy here. Mom has two categories: either it's getting packed in a box or gotten rid of. Seems to be about 50/50. I'm standing guard over my things. Mom called her human kids and told them to come get their stuff or it's getting tossed. I don't think they initially believed her until she made a video of her tossing a box into the dumpster and let them know that the dumpster was being carted away soon. Hahaha! Boy, that got them visiting pretty quickly.

Spirit: You two, get over here.
Cecil/Speedy G: Yes sir!
Spirit: I'll let you play with one of my squeakies if you stand guard while I go outside. Make sure Pooh Bear does not steal my squeakies!
Cecil/Speedy G: Yes sir!

Pooh Bear has been an asshole. He keeps stealing my squeakies and tells me that Mom threw them away.

Pooh Bear: That's Mr. Asshole to you!

I'm getting a little concerned. My stuff has not been packed yet and the garage is full of packed boxes that don't contain my stuff. I can't even walk in the garage without bonking myself on the boxes.

Now they're loading up the car for the drive to the new house AND MY STUFF IS NOT PACKED YET!

Spirit: MOM! My stuff!
Mary: *Don't worry, It'll all get packed in the morning before we leave.*

Mom and Dad packed us all in one big crate with our beds and some of my squeakies.

Spirit: Are we there yet?

Mary: *Sigh. We just pulled out of the garage. It's going to take us four days.*

I don't dare try to escape, even if I could. There's a lot of stuff in this car. Pooh's been eyeing my squeaky, and if I'm not careful, he'll lay down on them and pretend he can't move.

Pooh Bear: I don't want to disturb Speedy and Cecil. See how relaxed they are?

Spirit: Asshole.

These dogs are going to kill me. They keep telling Dad they have to pee. They don't, they just want to stop and look at different places. Oh look, a blade of grass, oh look a different blade of grass. At this rate, it's going to take four months to get to the new house. Apparently, their plan is to mark every rest stop between Connecticut and Washington.

OMG! I think I'm channeling Ricky! I just told Cecil that's not the way we do things. What's wrong with me? Stop it! They were being crazy in the hotel room. I get it, they're not seasoned travelers like me. All of this is new to them. They must be scared and a little stressed. I even gave Pooh one of my squeakies so he could relax a bit. Somebody take my temperature, I must be sick!

Two years later, we arrived at our destination.

Mary: *It was four days.*

This place smells different, yet the same. Different trees and grass, but very similar. I smelled Mom and Dad in the house when she brought us in. She made the boys go outside and run around and pee while I got to check out this new place without interference.

The floor feels cold!

Mary: *Tile floors.*

Spirit: Is that a fireplace? You didn't tell me we had a fireplace.

Mary: *I'll turn it on for you. And there's central AC, so you'll always be cool, no matter how hot it gets.*

Spirit: My bed is near the fireplace. Ooh the heat feels good on my hips and my head is on a cool tile floor. I could get used to this.

Now all we need is a little snow.

Chapter 25

2020 - Retirement

I didn't think I'd ever want to retire, but I see the allure.

This new place we're living in is so worth the four-day trip in a cramped car with my brothers. Can you imagine four days of Are We There Yet in stereo? I was so glad to have my own bed. Every time we stopped, I got all the news around the country. I mean rest stops are great, and I didn't even mind my brothers posting their travels as we made our way over to Washington.

But back to retirement. This home has tile floors, it always feels just a little bit cool. Then there's the fireplace. I never knew these existed. They're so warm! So, I can lie my head on the floor and point my achy hips toward the fireplace. I could do this 24/7.

For a while, Mom would take me out to teach, but honestly, getting in and out of the car was painful no matter how careful Mom was. So, I stopped traveling with her.

Besides, Dad is retired. He spends most of the day watching TV and puttering around while Mom works in her office. Sometimes I hang out in her office and help when she holds classes there, but man, that fireplace keeps calling me. Mom says I deserve to retire and live the good life. She said someone has to keep Dad company and out of her office.

Listen, that's a job in itself! Every time Dad gets up and looks like he's heading over to Mom's office instead of the kitchen, I pretend I have to pee and am having trouble getting up. Dad comes running over to help me get up and then, over to the stairs and then, wait for me. By the time I finish, he's forgotten what he wanted. Hahaha!

Mary: *Thank you.*

Even though Mom puts on my work bandana around the house, I was feeling a little left out since I'm no longer going to trade shows.. It's not the same. Yeah, Mom and Dad shower me with attention, but I'm not getting the love from everyone else. I was feeling like I'm being forgotten.

Well, Mom took care of that! It's getting a little exciting around here. She's in a bidding war with some people online because she wants this beautiful necklace made by Joleelee Creations for me. It's one of a kind. Just like me! It was a fundraiser for a good friend in the industry who got very sick. I'm told it's red with crystals and is very big and flashy. Just like me.

The bidding started at $5. But these ladies aren't playing as this auction is only open for a couple of hours. First bid was $30 and Mom went to $35, then someone countered with $40 and Mom went to $45. Too rich for her blood. Mom took out the first contender. But wait there's someone new now , and she went up to $60. Bye, Bye, Kristie. Mom just out bid you at $65. Go, Mom! I want this necklace.

Even my brothers are getting excited. Every time Mom shouts out the next bid along with her commentary, they all run around up and bark.

Dad came into the office and was wondering what the ruckus was. Mom sent him away and told him not to bother her, she was working. Hahaha! That's right, Dad. WE'RE WORKING. Working on getting this necklace that is!

Now there's another player in the game, and she's starting at $70. Mom is $75. Kris is $77. Is she slowing down? I hope so. This only costs $50. Mom had to finish up this auction at her hairdresser as she is now getting her hair done, and everyone at the salon is cheering her on. Mom is determined.

Marcus has joined us and is relaying the bidding from the salon.

$80
$85
$90
$95
$100

I gotta pee. Hey, Dad!
Neither one is giving up!
It's almost 5:00. It's going to end soon. Even though Mom had finished up her appointment, she couldn't leave! Not until the bidding was done.

$105
$110

AND MOM WON AT $111!!!!
So sorry, Kris. It's all mine. Marcus told us that the whole salon cheered.
Dad asked what took so long this time when she got home. And Mom blamed traffic. Hahaha!
It came a couple of weeks later, and it's huge. It hangs halfway down my chest. Mom says I

look elegant. And that I can wear it anytime I want. I asked my brothers how I looked since I couldn't see it.

Speedy G: It's so pretty. The red stands out against your white fur.

Cecil: It's you. It's sparkly

Pooh Bear: I like it. Hey Mom, where's mine?

Mary: *It's bigger than you. How about a bow tie instead?*

So now all of us are dressed in our finery and strutting around the house. But, to be clear, mine is the nicest.

Mom posted my photo all over Facebook and she read me all the comments. I feel so special. Thank you!!!

Once a month, Dad makes a trip out to see his mother and that makes Pooh Bear very happy. But he came home one time with another dog. Apparently, Dad's mom can no longer take care of him and now Mickey is part of our family.

Spirit: Welcome, Mickey. You two get over here and say hi to your new brother.

Cecil/Speedy G: Welcome Mickey!

Mickey: Thank you. I claim Dad.

Pooh Bear: Hahaha! You do that. Keep him away from my Mom.

Mickey: I like this Mom better than my first Mom.

Pooh Bear: I feel ya. She was my first Mom as well.

Chapter 26

Seizures and Declining Health

What the fuck just happened?!

One minute I'm sleeping on my bed and then, the next thing I know, I'm at the emergency vet's office and being poked and prodded. I feel weird. I'm told I've had a seizure. I don't know what that is.

> **Mary's note:** *Then I'll explain. Something triggered abnormal electrical activity in your brain sending a scrambled message to the muscles of your body. In short, you short circuited.*
>
> There are two different categories of seizures; the first is Idiopathic and the second is Symptomatic.
>
> **Idiopathic** is generally a genetic defect. Seizures begin at an early age and can be caused by Hydrocephalus, Juvenile hypoglycemia or any genetic endocrine or metabolic disorders. Idiopathic does not apply to you. You're nine.
>
> **Symptomatic** is caused by either a brain lesion or a specific disorder.
>
> If it is a specific disorder, there will be a trigger. A trigger is something that causes you to have a seizure such as any of the causes of the idiopathic variety that are not genetic in nature, poisoning, infectious agents, sudden blunt force trauma, brain infection, diabetes, or cancer.

Spirit: What about the full moon? I remember looking up in the sky wondering if I'll turn into a werewolf.

Mary: *What? No, you are not going to turn into a werewolf.*

Spirit: Bummer!

Mary: *All your blood work came back normal, so the vet is thinking it's probably a brain lesion. There is nothing we can do except to manage the occurrences.*

Spirit: Well, that sucks.

Mary: *There's more to learn about seizures. There are four stages. The first is the Prodome. That's the time before the seizure. There will be a subtle change in your mood or behavior.*

Spirit: I remember feeling weird. I felt kind of fuzzy, which is why I was wondering about the whole werewolf thing.

Mary: *The Aura is the start of the seizure. You might be restless or hyperactive.*

Spirit: I was definitely restless. I thought for certain it would be quick to turn into a werewolf.

Mary: *Dude, what is the fascination with werewolves?*

Spirit: Pooh Bear said not to look in the direction of the moon. That it was a full moon tonight. He said I would turn into a werewolf. I thought it would be cool to be a werewolf. All I did was turn my head towards the sky. Wait a minute….. Ooh, I'm gonna mess with him when I get home.

Mary: *The Ictus is the actual seizure. You had no control over your body. Good thing you were on your bed so that you banged your head against the cushion rather than the floor.*

Spirit: I don't remember that.

Mary: *The Post-Ictal is after the seizure is over. Your behavior may change. We don't know what that looks like since we just loaded you into the car and called the emergency hospital to let them know we're on our way. Let's go home. I bet you're tired.*

Oh. I'm tired alright. Tired of Pooh Bear and his shenanigans. I'm going to take a nap in the car and get back at him when I get home.

Cecil/Speedy G: Pooh come quick! Spirit's home. Are you okay? We were so worried about you.

Spirit: I was turning into a werewolf!

Pooh Bear: Wait, what? I was joking.

Spirit: No, you were correct. I looked in the direction of a full moon, now I'm a werewolf! Good thing Mom got me to the hospital in time to reverse it.

Pooh Bear: Oh, good.

Spirit: This time.

Pooh Bear: This time?

Spirit: That's right! Something might set me off and then, I turn into a werewolf. You should hide if that happens.

Pooh Bear: Like a full moon?

Spirit: Oh no, we're past that. More like something pissing me off, like stealing my squeakies.

Pooh Bear: I'll be right back!

Spirit: You two come here.

Cecil/Speedy G: Yes sir!

Spirit: I'm not really a werewolf, I'm just messing with Pooh Bear.

Cecil/Speedy G: We know!

Pooh Bear: I found all your squeakies that you lost! I collected and saved them for you!

After having several seizures now, Mom and Dad are less freaked out by them and most of the time, I know it's coming. The worst part is afterwards. I'm compelled to walk around my deck for hours. My hips hurt. This is terrible.

But the good news is that Pooh is no longer stealing my squeakies. Also, because I feel so hot after a seizure, I now have my own personal industrial fan that blows on my bed.

Seizures and Declining Health | 109

Chapter 27

2021 - Last Days

I'm back from the vet's office yet again, and they told Mom I have an anal tumor that can't be removed because of my seizures. It's going to grow until it bursts. So now, Mom is checking my gums every couple of hours to see if they have gone pale, which would indicate that the tumor has burst.

Time to have a discussion with my brothers.

Spirit: Listen guys, my time is almost up.
Cecil/Speedy G: We don't want you to go! We love you.
Pooh Bear: I'm sorry for always stealing your squeakies.
Mickey: What's going on? Where are you going?
Pooh Bear: Keep up, Mickey. Spirit is going to die soon. He'll be joining all our brothers and sisters who have left us.
Spirit: You need to be strong for Mom and Dad. Pooh, you can have all my squeakies.
Mickey: What about me? Can I have one? You have the best squeakies.
Spirit: Pooh will share.
Pooh: I will?
Spirit: Yes, you will.

This is going to be difficult for Mom. I wish she could see everyone that is waiting for me to help me cross over. Ricky, Baby, Reno, Marcus, and Kira have all been here for the last couple of days. AND my first Mom is here too!!! I think Mom would have an easier time if she could see them knowing my support system is in place.

Kira: Mom will not let you suffer. It's why she keeps checking your gums. She doesn't want to let you go a minute sooner than she has to.

Spirit: My Mom is here. Do you see her?! I never thought I'd see my first Mom again.

Mom: *I've been waiting for you.*

Ricky: It's time son. I nudged her in her dreams. She's going to jump out of bed and check on you shortly.

Marcus: Let's go, Baby. Time to wake up Mom.

Mom had to make the decision today. I'm done and it's time to move on to my guardian stage. I'll still be around as A Spirit. Just not physically. I trust her to know I can't go on. She loves me enough to let me go even though it's going to hurt her heart.

Mary's final notes: *I've been blessed over the years with my canine companions. All of them have left a lasting impression on my soul. I could write a book about all of them, but this one is about Spirit. Spirit was my blind (glaucoma), toothless (distemper), bad hips (puppy mill) Siberian Husky. Despite his health, the one thing he was, was happy. He was true to his nature and a conscientious working dog. He traveled with me across the country, being an ambassador, a clown, all while helping me teach pet first aid to pet professionals and pet owners alike. He was always up for fun. The creative groomers at trade shows had their way with him, and he loved every minute of it. When I lost Spirit, I didn't just lose a traveling buddy. I lost a colleague. Spirit wasn't just a "member" of the family. He was family.*

Acknowledgments

Spirit and I would like to thank the following as this book could not have been written without their help.

Chris Anthony, Dr, Sacheen Mobley, and Anjie Coates. We love you.

To Ernesto, a wonderful dog dad, great encourager, and good sport.

Dogs with special needs hold a special place in my heart. Spirit was not my first special needs, and he won't be the last. These pups do well when the owner has a good support system in place. We would like to be part of that support system. Come find us on Facebook at https://www.facebook.com/aspiriteddog.

www.ingramcontent.com/pod-product-compliance
Lightning Source LLC
Chambersburg PA
CBHW042138290426
44110CB00002B/51